Penguin Education

Penguin Education Specials
General Editor Willem van der Eyken

The Multi-Racial School
Edited by Julia McNeal and Margaret Rogers

The Multi-Racial School
A Professional Perspective
Edited by Julia McNeal and
Margaret Rogers

With a Foreword by Dipak Nandy

Penguin Books

Penguin Books Ltd, Harmondsworth,
Middlesex, England
Penguin Books Inc, 7110 Ambassador Road,
Baltimore, Md 21207, USA
Penguin Books Australia Ltd,
Ringwood, Victoria, Australia

First published 1971
Reprinted 1972
Copyright © Julia McNeal, Margaret Rogers and contributors, 1971

Made and printed in Great Britain by
Cox & Wyman Ltd,
London, Reading and Fakenham
Set in Intertype Plantin

Contents

Foreword
Dipak Nandy

Through the 1950s Britain acquired a coloured population in, so to speak, a fit of absence of mind. Since the process of immigration was not planned, it was on the whole no one's responsibility in particular to anticipate and to provide for the foreseeable consequences of the process. Indeed, the policy-makers of the time breathed an air of ample and generous liberalism of which we can say with hindsight that, although magnificent, it was not a policy nor the basis for an effective one.

The failure to have a policy meant that, in the field of education, schools and teachers were left to recognize and then respond to the problems and challenges of a multi-racial society on their own. Two further consequences flowed from this initial failure. In the absence of discussion on the likely shape of a multi-racial society, teachers and educationists adopted the language of the market place – because there was no other language available – in describing their situation: they were dealing with 'the immigrant problem'. More and more a way of talking developed in which the very presence of coloured children was held to constitute a 'problem'. Furthermore, because the situation was dealt with piecemeal, we developed an obsession with pseudo-problems while neglecting to notice the real problems. The obsession with pseudo-problems and the neglect of the real problems were parasitic one upon another.

There were at least four distinct problems which were seldom separated out. There was first the problem of teaching English to non-English speaking immigrant children. For this task the educational system – and in particular the schools to which the children were consigned by virtue of the pattern of residential settlement – proved inadequate. Secondly, there was the problem of helping immigrant children to adjust to a new society, to a different relationship between home and school and a different atmosphere within the schools. But the absence of teachers trained to teach English as a second language meant that, in their necessary preoccupation with the language problem, schools were seldom able to provide the equally necessary attention that adjustment to a new life and a new style of life required. Thirdly, there was the problem of understanding what it meant to be a child belonging to a minority group, marked out by colour and sometimes by culture and religion.

Official policy on this question was at first strictly assimilationist. The Second Report of the Commonwealth Immigrants Advisory Committee declared:

A national system of education must aim at producing citizens who can take their place in society properly equipped to exercise rights and perform duties the same as those of other citizens. If their parents were brought up in another culture and another tradition, children should be encouraged to respect it, but a national system cannot be expected to perpetuate the different values of immigrant groups.

The stern school-marmish tone of voice in those sentences does, however, fail to engage with some important questions. To what extent do the majority of our schools manage to perform these laudable functions for *native* children, let alone the newcomers? To what extent is so strict an emphasis on what, in the language of the marketplace, is known as 'learning the British way of life' really compatible with that respect for the culture and tradition of the parents which is also held to be desirable? And, of course, there is no recognition that a child from a minority group brings with him to school a background of experience – of racial prejudice and of discrimination – which will require special attention from his teachers if they are to elicit any kind of a real response from the child. Although the assimilationist fervour declined through the 1960s, it was not replaced by any more profound and positive an understanding of the educational and psychological needs of children from minority groups.

And this linked with the fourth problem: what were the educational needs of a multi-racial society? The phrase 'multi-racial society' can be used in its descriptive, and trivial, sense to refer to a society which simply happens to have more than one ethnic group in it. But in its non-trivial sense it must refer to an *ideal* of society rather than to the facts of its ethnic composition, and it must refer to a state of affairs which (in Roy Jenkins's rightly celebrated definition of 'integration') entails 'equal opportunity, accompanied by cultural diversity, in an atmosphere of mutual tolerance'. Now such a state of affairs has, as an ideal, its attendant difficulties, and it is arguable to what extent the components are mutually compatible. But what is certain is that if such an ideal were possible, it would assuredly not be realized automatically.

So here, in considering the problems which schools faced in dealing with an increasing number of coloured immigrant children, we are forced up against the question of the relation of education to society. For my part I do not think that it is easy to improve upon Cardinal Newman when he writes, in *The Idea of a University*:

If then a practical end must be assigned to a university course, I say it is that of training good members of society. Its art is the art of social life, and its end fitness for the world.

Nor do I think that he would have been unhappy to represent that as the purpose of education as such. But if that is what education is for, then we have to ask: what kind of society is it which we are training good members of? The point of the question is that a multi-racial society requires an educational system which is responsive to the value of cultural diversity, that such a response does not arise automatically but requires a positive determination to seek it, and that an excessive preoccupation with bringing racially or culturally alien children up to some unspecified British Standards Institute specification does not help to produce that kind of responsiveness. And of course it follows that an education responsive to the needs of a multi-racial society involves not only immigrant children, but also native; not only black children, but also white; not only multi-racial schools, but also schools which are unlikely to see a non-white face in the foreseeable future.

These were the problems we faced. Official policy did not sufficiently distinguish them, when indeed it noticed that they were there. Not surprisingly, teacher and schools faced with new demands for which they had neither the skills nor the resources saw the arrival of coloured immigrant children in their class-rooms as 'the problem'. I do not suggest that teachers were, as a profession, responsible for the misdefinition of the real problem. The real responsibility lies with the policy of *laissez-faire* which characterized the whole field of race relations and immigration, and it is as well to remind ourselves that *laissez-faire* is not the *absence* of policy so much as a policy *not* to have a policy.

Underneath the issues which a multi-racial society raises for the educational system lies the basic issue of what our educational system as such is good for. Here, as elsewhere, the arrival of coloured children drew attention to and highlighted deficiencies in our institutions themselves. Just at the time that we were preoccupied with the linguistic handicaps of culturally alien children, Professor Bernstein and his colleagues were mapping out the linguistic handicaps of native working-class children. The inability of schools to meet adequately the needs of newcomers turned out to be an extension of their inability to meet the needs of deprived children – of whatever kind. Sometimes we took an unhealthy, zoological interest in the 'cultural background' of immigrant children – as though they were a new species of flora and fauna deposited in our midst – in order to account for their difficulties in school, when a simple inspection of their housing condition, which they share with many native children, would have provided a sufficient explanation. But the point that has emerged abundantly in the last decade is that knowing what life is like in the Caribbean (valuable as that is in promoting a respect for cultural diversity) is still no substitute for knowing what life in an overcrowded house in, say, Islington or Handsworth is like.

It is no doubt a coincidence, but a formidable coincidence for all that, that the growth of our awareness of the problems of race relations took place at the same time as we were beginning to rediscover, through a sequence of massive reports – Crowther, Newsom, Robbins, Plowden – the nature and extent of the deficiencies of the educational system as such. But given the coincidence it would be negligent to overlook the moral that follows from it. Whatever special strategies education for a multi-racial society may require, they will be ineffective except against the background of a more effective and humane strategy for education as such. If we will the means – a deficient and segregated educational system – we make our small contribution towards willing the end – a deficient and segregated society. Whether, in such a society, the lines of segregation coincide with colour, or whether colour and class lines criss-cross, is, in terms of the human waste involved, relatively unimportant. What is important is that there will be little hope of achieving equality of opportunity, tolerance and a respect for cultural diversity for minority groups in society if those virtues are lacking in social relationships as a whole.

This is the background against which, I suggest, the ensuing essays should be seen. In the absence of an official policy and of agreed guidelines, each of the contributors had to work out a strategy of his or her own. What follows, therefore, is not a catalogue of 'problems', but sober accounts of what teachers and heads have done to meet the challenge of multi-racial schools – schools which are in some instances deprived schools as well. It is not a shopping list of what *can* be done – it is a record of what *has been done*, sometimes in unpropitious settings.

Our original intention, in commissioning these essays from teachers whose energies can only uneasily be diverted from education to writing about education, was to provide simply a record of what has been done, *pour encourager les autres*. But it would be a gross underestimation of the cumulative impact of these contributions to think that they do not raise much broader issues concerning the relationship (or lack of it) of education and society, in particular of our educational system and our society.

The Runnymede Trust
April 1971

Introduction
Julia McNeal and Margaret Rogers

This book will make some contribution, we hope, to a professional dialogue about the methods and aims of teaching in multi-racial schools, and about the contribution which all schools could make to our multi-racial society. Blueprints would be out of place for a number of reasons. First (and least important) because multi-racial schools differ greatly in their racial and national composition, and in the kinds of mixed communities they serve. Secondly, and more important, because they differ in the talents and interests they can draw upon among staff and pupils. Any breakthrough in standards is bound to be dependent on such 'accidental' factors – given raw material with which a creative teacher can build. Thirdly, good practices in schools (like other institutions) are not fixed – they can end with a change of staff, or they can develop, be discarded or expanded. Finally blueprints do not usually provide enough information about the way new methods should be handled if they are to succeed – in every single one of the specific projects described in this book, the way in which they are introduced and put into practice is all important.

But there is one assumption behind the book about which we have no doubts, and that is the need to develop a rationale about the factors likely to be at work in multi-racial schools, and the kind of general skills and materials which teachers in them need. This is a controversial assumption. There are many teachers who work in multi-racial schools who prefer to see them (if we ignore the presence of the small minority of wholly non-English-speaking pupils) as English schools with perhaps a higher proportion of children who are in one way or another 'deprived' but whose problems are essentially the same as those of deprived English children. This view has probably gained strength as the number of English-born 'immigrants' has increased, the number of new arrivals fallen, and the language difficulties of immigrant pupils apparently become less severe. It has a lot to recommend it – particularly in contrast to an earlier view, still current, which treated the problems of multi-racial schools solely as imported problems.

A visit to two good primary schools, one with at least half its pupils of immigrant parentage, the other wholly white, might reveal little difference in the character, the atmosphere, between the two schools: small-group teaching, art work round the walls, nature collections, mathematics materials, groups watching television, small remedial groups at work, singing classes probably working on the same songs, much the same books in the libraries. Just because one school is multi-racial will not mean that the teachers lose their main interest in particular subjects, and the developments in them which are quite general. If one looked a little more closely at what lay behind the differing climates in these schools, one would probably find that it was partly dependent on good administration; partly on subject matter and materials which are common to many primary schools; and partly on certain cultural choices which were made by the staff – the books, the songs, the themes in art work. Indeed the extent to which a good multi-racial school appears 'different' in its superficial aspect depends a great deal on whether the teachers allow the various cultural inheritances of the children to be expressed; it is the teacher's decision.

There are reasons why some teachers do not want their schools to be described in any way which marks them out as 'different' either because they do not like working in a multi-racial school, or perhaps more commonly because of the ignorance of colleagues who equate 'multi-racial' with 'inferior', 'immigrant' with 'problems'. George Meredith refers in chapter 4 explicitly to the 'loss of prestige' felt by staff in his school as it became multi-racial – part of an acute problem of school morale.

It is not pleasant to become an object of pity, particularly when this is linked with a kind of prurient interest which often accompanies ignorance about multi-racial schools (the concept of deprivation can also call forth this kind of attitude). In favouring a professional dialogue about work in multi-racial schools we are not proposing, for example, collective evocation of the inad-

equacies of immigrant learners, the inadequacy of education services in the countries of origin, nor for an exchange of anecdotes
about goings on in individual familes – possibly disguised as 'case
histories'. What we are proposing is *an analysis of the educational needs of children, including white English children, in
multi-racial schools*, and the corresponding *resource needs
of teachers in those schools*. This is no more and no less than
the kind of rational approach one would like to see in all
schools.

In this book, each of the contributors deals with a different
measure or set of measures which were undertaken to solve the
school's problems, as these were defined and redefined over time
by the head and staff. In some cases, the teachers at least started
out by perceiving themselves and the school to be in a crisis
situation; in other cases, however, what were defined as problems
reflected the teachers' judgement about what they needed to improve their teaching, or about the proper role of their school
within its community. For example, in chapter 1, the language
centre was developed in response to a situation in which many
children were failing to make any progress within the conventional school organization and the training and resources
geared to an English school population. In the second chapter,
however, the links with parents were built up *not* in order to
solve a crisis in the school, but to increase support for the pupils,
and to solve a problem in the community outside – the
indifference and hostility which existed between different
national and racial groups.

But despite the variations in the state of school morale and
other factors, the contributors describe schools which share certain difficulties in common. In terms of the proportion of 'immigrant pupils' which they have, all these schools (except Margaret
Nandy's) represent only a minority of multi-racial schools. Most
mixed-race, mixed-nationality schools have far fewer pupils of
overseas parentage. In most multi-racial schools, therefore, the
minorities may impinge less on normal routines than they do in
the schools we chose for this book. This does not mean that the
same problems do not exist, merely that they are less likely to be
perceived. Certainly we believe that when the complex variables
at work in multi-racial schools are spelled out, they are quite

recognizable to teachers of multi-racial classes, whatever the 'density' of the immigrant population of their schools.

What then are the most important factors affecting teachers' work in multi-racial schools?

It may be helpful to consider first the sort of school which would be the exact opposite of a multi-racial one. This would be typically a school serving a highly stable residential area, a community all of whom shared the same language, the same kind of upbringing, the same expectations about school and society. It might be a high or a low achieving school – a private boarding school catering for the elite, or an EPA school in a traditional working-class area. By contrast, the most characteristic fact about the typical urban multi-racial school is its *diversity* – diversity of languages, diversity of expectations about school and society. It serves an unstable, fragmented community. It is a school whose children come from many different cultural backgrounds, in most cases not shared by the teachers, and to a greater or lesser extent unfamiliar to them. Of course each school has its own, institutional, 'culture' – its rules, its hierarchy and so forth. Sometimes this can completely overwhelm the home culture of the pupils, as generations of colonial teachers would testify, to take an extreme example. But in the homogenous school, there is, beneath the school culture a wider source of reference points shared by teachers and pupils. The teachers may be from the local community, or have acquiried an intimate knowledge of it through their work.

It is obvious that our counter-example, the homogeneous school, presents a somewhat idealist picture of school life; it is doubtful whether it accurately describes the situation in very many of our urban schools today. For example, it would not apply to any school with a high staff turnover; it would not apply to any school with a class of fourth-year leavers or any group considered 'unteachable'; it would not apply to schools with many drug takers, or with pupils who are promiscuous or frequently before the courts, although one can think of schools where the teachers had and have considerable understanding of their deviant school population. Then there is the work of Bernstein and of the Institute of Education which suggests that there is a linguistic barrier between the language used by pupils from unskilled manual working-class homes and the language used and demanded by the teachers and by the education system. All of this suggests that the problems thrown up by multi-racial schools should not be seen as unique, or isolated ones, but only more obvious cases of problems which are posed in white schools and by white society. In fact, there may be clues in the multi-racial situation about these wider problems. This emerges clearly from the contributions of Hugh Cunningham and Margaret Nandy to this book.

The most obvious diversities which affect teaching in multi-racial schools, particularly where they still include children from overseas, or born in Britain to families in which English is not normally spoken, are those of language, of cultural – or to be more precise, moral – training, and of educational experience. Classes are likely to contain learners whose mother tongue is not English, learners whose mother tongue is a variant of English and those whose mother tongue is English but certainly not 'school English'. Within all three categories there may be a wide range of competence. Diversity, then, both in the type of linguistic difficulty and its severity, within one class. All these difficulties may lead to breakdowns in understanding between pupils and teacher, which can affect not only the 'information–knowledge' working areas, but also the whole pupil–teacher relationship, including its more informal and personal aspects, which are an essential element of classroom atmosphere. Teachers will say 'I can't get on their wavelength', 'There's always someone who doesn't understand', 'You can't joke some of them out of their moods – they don't understand the humour', etc. The various religious and national groups within a school have their own moral codes, which are often unfamiliar and even unknown to their teachers. They may interfere with many of the practical arrangements of school life: dress for gym, co-educational activities, food and so on; and again, they can lead to mis-understandings which block the development of good pupil–teacher relationships.

It would be a mistake, of course, to regard every detail of moral and religious codes of immigrant groups as fixed. There has naturally been, on the one hand, a good deal of flexibility and adaptation to British norms, and, on the other hand, in some cases an increasing commitment to traditional practices during a community's development in Britain. The various encapsulated written accounts of aspects of Islam, Sikhism, Hinduism, which are now increasingly available to students and teachers, can only be used as starting points, not as substitutes for live contact. This underlines the value of the work done in multi-racial schools, primary and secondary, to increase communication with immigrant parents. But again, as Hugh Cunningham suggests in his chapter, once a school begins to analyse its knowledge of the culture of its pupils and their parents, it may well be surprised at the gaps in its understanding of its *English* pupils.

Language differences and differences in cultural background of a traditional kind – these are two of the obvious characteristics of multi-racial schools. There are others which may endure even if and when teachers become highly trained language teachers, and when they have built up as good a knowledge of immigrant home background as of English home background. Many of the pupils in multi-racial schools – sometimes all of them – are members of minority groups, because of their race, colour or national origin, or, in the case of some, because of their social position (e.g. 'problem families'). This minority status exists for them independently of their linguistic and cultural differences and affects the way in which they will regard the school as well as the wider society. In the case of 'immigrant pupils' it means that many features of life become problematic which, for the majority, are taken for granted: do we have a legal right to remain in Britain? will it be safe and wise to do so? and with a sense of security? what reception will we get from white authorities? will the teachers be prejudiced against us? Most of these pupils are under stress in some way or other. They are marginal children, straddling two cultures, often two languages or dialects. In school, they are very often faced with an additional 'school culture' and 'school language' to master. Their attitudes towards questions of race may range from self-hatred, desire for assimilation, to black self-assertion, political black militancy and hatred of whites. In some schools, stresses can produce explosive reactions or extreme withdrawal. In others, teachers may not notice any observable signs of stress among their minority pupils, and the observable problem may well be the hostility and offensiveness of white pupils. It may be a matter of urgency to do something to improve the state of race relations within a school. Or it may be possible for teachers to ignore race relations altogether. But, although possible, it would be quite unrealistic, because teachers are seen as protagonists whether they accept this or not, and their indifference noted as much as any overt signs of interest. If they do attempt a positive response, teachers are in a weak position of having no obvious shared experience to draw on: nor have they been trained to deal with stresses arising from race relations.

Despite these stresses, multi-racial schools are not always less disciplined than homogeneous schools, immigrant pupils do not necessarily display more problems than white English children in multi-racial schools. Recent research in the West Midlands found that the proportion of Caribbean pupils who seemed to their teachers to show signs of difficult behaviour was not much greater than the proportion of white English children, the greatest difference being in signs of withdrawal among infants.* However, what teachers should expect in multi-racial schools serving EPA or borderline EPA areas is a high proportion of all children – white and black – with emotional and learning problems. This relative concentration of problems is due to the nature of the area served by the school. They are areas of furnished tenancies, that ever shrinking sector in the major cities where jobs are available, into which must be crammed all those who do not qualify for council housing, and who cannot afford unfurnished tenancies, or ownership of newer one-family homes. They are areas of bad shared housing, lack of gardens or communal space, lack of nursery schools and play groups, lack of sports facilities, lack of arts facilities, lack of book shops, lack of legal services. They are typically unstable, as families move out in search of better and/or cheaper housing, although this movement may well remain within borough boundaries, and even be accompanied by loyalties to the neighbourhood in some places. From such areas all children come to school handicapped compared with suburban children from post-war housing estates. In

* Schools Council Working Paper 29, 'Teaching English to West Indian children: the research stage of the project', Evans-Methuen Educational, Schools Council Publications, 1970.

a multi-racial primary school in an EPA area, the most backward group will probably include as many English as immigrant children. For this reason many teachers remain hostile to the idea of considering immigrants as a distinct group. Yet even in the matter of housing need, which cuts across many groups, there are certain differences between groups worthwhile for teachers to consider. The facts are that very bad housing is both more general and more enduring among the immigrant population in boroughs with bad housing problems.

One specific example illustrates this. In seven inner London boroughs in 1966 these were the percentages of various groups living in overcrowded conditions (1961 overcrowding index) and the percentages sharing accommodation.

	Overcrowding	Sharing
English	5%	39%
Irish	27%	60%
Cypriot	36%	62%
Indian, Pakistani	32%	59%
Jamaican	47%	82%
Rest of Caribbean	59%	84%

The study from which these figures are drawn concluded:

Between 1961 and 1966 the main coloured immigrant groups showed very little overall improvement in their housing conditions. While access to household facilities improved and there was movement out of the least advantageous sector of the housing market (renting furnished) their level of overcrowding remained very high and the proportion sharing showed a slight increase. In contrast the period has been one of improvement from English residents of these boroughs and, while comparisons are difficult, it would seem that the coloured immigrants were being left even further behind as the general level of housing amenity has risen.*

In an EPA primary school there may be little difference between the housing conditions of immigrant and English pupils. In schools serving areas with new council housing, and in sec-

* Nicholas Deakin and associates, *Colour, Citizenship and British Society*, Panther, 1970.

ondary schools with wide catchment areas, the discrepancies are likely to be much greater. If bad housing has a bad effect on educational performance, and if schools devise ways of compensating, for example, for the lack of privacy and lack of space in the homes (through play centres, or time and place for quiet individual work) then it seems this would affect a very high proportion indeed of the pupils of immigrant origin – in some places, almost an entire local population.

The housing figures (just one example drawn from very extensive and varied research into the field) suggest that most immigrant families share with the most deprived sections of the English almost impossibly harsh living conditions. But what about other factors which are often taken to affect children's performance in school, for example, parents' occupation? Here the evidence shows that immigrant groups as a whole cannot simply be fitted into a mould prepared for deprived English groups. Immigrants may be doing jobs which the English would not take, but these jobs cover a wide range of levels of skill. Again, to take a few examples: West Indians in Britain (in common with most immigrants groups) have roughly the same proportion of *skilled* manual workers as the English population (roughly 40 per cent in London, more in the Midlands). This is sometimes forgotten when their over-representation in labouring and semi-skilled jobs is noted (very roughly 25 per cent in each, compared with about 10 per cent to 20 per cent of the English). On the negative side there is one problem which seems to affect Caribbean children proportionately more than other groups – the sheer number of women at work. Over 60 per cent of Caribbean women are working (mostly in blue-collar jobs, a quarter in the Health Service including a significant proportion of trained nurses). This compares with about 40 per cent of the total female population. Measures to provide adequate pre-school experience for children of working mothers might well therefore have a particularly dramatic effect upon future Caribbean pupils. The reality of the situation in a London education priority area is nicely described by Winifred Bindley in this book.

If we turn to the next largest group of 'immigrant pupils', the Indians, there is in some ways an even more varied picture. In London far more men and women have white-collar jobs than the general population; in the Midlands, however, this is an almost completely working-class group, with 30 per cent in labouring jobs. On the other hand (in 1966 when these figures were collected) very few Indian women outside London went out to work, and most young children therefore presumably were cared for by their mothers at home.*

Apart from these facts about occupations, there are, of course, a number of less tangible, less easily described factors about the family background of children in 'deprived areas': relationships between parents and children, father and mother, the family's bonds with relatives, with others from the same ethnic, cultural or religious background, and with neighbours. Here again, most familiar generalizations about immigrant groups are un-satisfactory, and it would be unwise for anyone not deeply fam-iliar with a locality and individual families to hazard any. It would, however, be wrong and unfortunate if teachers merely assumed that immigrant pupils and their parents only pose prob-lems. They suffer various kinds of difficulty: they are, with the exception of Indians in London, predominantly working-class groups, and therefore share certain problems with two-thirds of the British population – in particular, an education system whose methods and rewards tend to favour middle-class pupils. (For some reading on class and education, see p. 153.) For a number of reasons however they do not share as yet in the access to council housing which is fairly typical of working-class families in the conurbations. In addition, the black groups suffer the manifold forms of racial prejudice and discrimination experienced in their history, and their economic and personal life in Britain. On top of this, a high proportion of immigrant families live in deprived areas, sharing their disadvantages with all the residents. To these areas they bring many strengths. One in particular is highly rel-evant to teachers. Despite the difficult circumstances from which most immigrant pupils enter school, they have brought with them a positive, not to say avid, regard for education. The blight of demoralization and apathy which afflicts large numbers of the

*E. J. B. Rose and associates, *Colour and Citizenship*, Oxford University Press, 1967, ch. 13. A comparative account of household budgeting and general standard of living of immigrant groups in Birmingham is available in chapter 14.

English pupils in deprived schools has not yet completely enveloped immigrant pupils. This is a positive factor which ought to be able to be used to fashion a sound educational policy. But it will continue only as long as schools seem to be providing opportunities that their pupils seek from their education.

So far we have outlined very briefly four factors which affect the teaching situation quite fundamentally in multi-racial schools:

1. Varied languages and range of competence in each.
2. Cultural differences between pupil and teacher, teacher and parents.
3. Race relations – a complex set of factors involving not only group relations within school, but every minority child's view of himself.
4. Deprivation of housing, income, environment leading to deprivation of family experience, and affecting the whole development of the child.

Each of these factors may be more or less noticeable to teachers in their various schools, but no one can say which, if any, are the more vital. None of the teaching problems thrown up by these four factors is absolutely new to the English education system, but in multi-racial schools they are combined in a form and on a scale which makes these schools unique. Moreover, although there are clues to understanding problems of multi-racial schools in problems of class conflict, and the failure of the education system to offer very much to many working-class pupils, there were no *solutions* in this area which multi-racial schools could borrow during the past ten years when they have been so desperately needed. Techniques, materials and rationale were lacking for problems of social class in school as much as for problems of racial or national group. More recently programmes addressed to the deprived child and to immigrant groups are being produced at the same time: e.g. 'Breakthrough to Literacy' and 'Teaching English to West Indian Children'. Both have much to offer all schools with a literacy problem. In many areas, problems of multi-racial schools were in fact quite new to the teachers.

Teachers come to this situation unprepared by their training and ill-equipped by the available materials. Colleges are beginning to provide optional courses in the teaching of English as a second language, usually for absolute beginners, as well as some courses in 'cultural background' and in race relations. All such training should be evaluated against the high teacher-turnover in the multi-racial areas. Those experienced teachers who do a great deal of in-service training are often alarmed at the way new techniques are grasped and applied as universal panaceas in the absence of a really thorough analysis of needs. There are Schools Council projects in progress or in production which individually have relevance to some parts and some age levels of multi-racial schools. But in most schools the organizational skills required to use these new materials to best advantage in the complex school situation have not yet been developed – may indeed be not even recognized as a requirement. Moreover, even if the new materials came to be incorporated into the curriculum of most schools which would benefit from them, they would still remain only a tiny part of the daily diet of standard texts, including new texts, in standard subjects. The ordinary subject teachers, who may not be concerned with language teaching, compensatory teaching or social studies, are very much on their own. If they feel that they can no longer teach their subject as they have developed it, that their curriculum aims are no longer relevant, they have nowhere obvious to turn for support in rethinking their work. Texts for all subject areas are produced with the English learner and mostly English middle-class culture in mind. For example, no subject texts have parallel materials at difference linguistic competence levels, a minimum requirement for most multi-racial groups. The same generally applies to other teaching media (tapes, visual aids, etc.). Few, if any, texts or materials reflect a pluralist society. Such texts as do exist are often unknown by most teachers, e.g. those on the history of the children's country of origin as seen through the eyes of their inhabitants – not through English eyes. Not all 'heros' in multi-racial schools should be white. This lack of relevant texts is likely to freeze the teacher's approach into an assimilationist mould, whether or not he or she has even thought about the issue.

Each of the contributors to this book addresses himself or herself to different aspects of life in multi-racial schools, and in most cases the work described is completely school-based. That is, although the schools benefited from extra staff or financial resources under various government programmes, they had no intellectual support from institutions outside their schools, and the specific materials required were not, at least initially, commercially available. (The two exceptions were Margaret Nandy, whose work was developed as part of a Nuffield project, and Doreen Manley, who worked from the Birmingham language centre, although her methods were entirely her own.) Three of the contributors describe how their schools reacted as communities to the experience of becoming multi-racial. In all three cases, the pattern which seems to have occurred was one of initial loss of control, followed by a continuing pattern of change in organization and curriculum and of evaluation. In one school (a primary school) a fairly definite form of organization, centred on a flexible language unit, seemed to offer long-term benefits to staff and pupils; in the two secondary-school examples, the story so far ends on a note of dissatisfaction and self-criticism – further changes are clearly recognized, but have yet to take root in the schools. In two of the primary schools, a series of small-scale measures together seem to indicate a total approach to relationships, between staff and parent, and staff and pupils, which not only depends upon teachers' personalities, but is much harder to define than adminstrative arrangements. It may be, as we discuss later, that before we come to 'good practices' we should discuss the kind of personality which teachers need for successful work in multi-racial schools, the kind of broad human education which teachers should be getting, the attitudes which should be required in candidates for jobs in multi-racial schools.

However, this book was put together on the assumption that in the present situation, when these special requirements are not forthcoming, there are certain positive practical measures which can fairly easily be defined, and which can at least make schools which seem difficult to teachers more interesting and hopeful places to work in. In any consideration by teacher groups of the difficulties of work in their schools, the measures described in this book are offered for discussion as possible or part solutions.

Language

The language unit (centre) was developed to cater for pupils with a wide variety of needs and different levels of competence, not just non-English speakers, not just beginners. It became clear that it could help English, and not necessarily just immigrant pupils. The language teacher used intensive oral work, in dialogue and drama, between pairs and groups of pupils themselves; she worked closely with subject teachers so that they too provided language drills, and subject and language learning became one. In our example, this worked well for non-academic subjects. For academic subjects – mathematics, history, science – more detailed planning and more work on texts would be needed. Publishers could usefully be involved. In Hugh Cunningham's school (chapter 8) not only did subject teachers take on special language tuition of non-English-speaking pupils, but *all* teachers became more language-conscious, and this was seen as a crucial feature of teaching in multi-racial schools.

Contact with parents

A variety of approaches was employed to reach the maximum number of parents. There was no appointment system, and for special meetings toddlers and babies were welcomed. Parents helped regularly in the classroom, and on weekly school visits; whole families came on seaside and pantomime outings. A joint parent–teacher dressmaking class reversed the normal status position – in it the parents became teachers, and the teachers learners. Most contacts were established in school time, not in teachers' free time.

There were two clear aims: to inform immigrant parents in particular about the school's educational methods, and so reduce conflicts between home and school demands on children; and to play a part in improving local community relations, by breaking down the isolation between different racial and national groups. In an unstable community, the school was seen as being in a specially favourable position to do this.

At the secondary level, both head teachers agreed that special efforts should be used to contact parents from overseas, and this was regarded as more difficult because of cultural differences and, equally important, because of bad community relations locally. In one case, fairly successful results came from a series of home visits made by pupils themselves, LEA school liaison officers, the head and some of the staff. In the other case, a special community liaison worker was appointed. The kind of reality which can be given to this liaison function between the local community and teachers had still to be fully developed at the time of writing.

Schools and deprived children

The general approach in both teaching and organization was child-centred and flexible – an approach common in many infant schools. This approach was informed by a special sensitivity to a whole range of handicaps suffered by the pupils, which were affecting their work. Three main examples of this were: first, the accumulation of very detailed information about children, so that teachers and head-teacher were aware, for example, of the child's family situation, medical history, diet, and any other points thought relevant. Acquiring this knowledge was not left to chance, and contact with social welfare departments was maintained; secondly, attempts to compensate for handicaps were very varied: provision of experience; provision of talk about children's experience by having many adult helpers, and encouraging sufficient time for listening to children; the play centre; milk available throughout the morning for children who had missed breakfast; and thirdly, school organization was flexible enough to permit stable relationships to develop between teacher and pupil; in some cases a relationship was expected to take several years to develop and benefit the child.

Ability grouping

Both secondary heads moved strongly away from streaming, and towards mixed-ability grouping, as their schools became increasingly multi-racial: the diversity of educational needs in the schools, and the large numbers of pupils who appeared as 'backward' by conventional English standards, made streaming seem increasingly unreal and unmanageable. At the same time, one school provided a 'primary-school department' for basic education. There were two other powerful reasons for the moves away from streaming: firstly, the bad effect upon race relations in school of having an 'all black' 'C' stream or remedial class, particularly when there was little movement out of such groupings. Secondly, the bad effect on motivation to learn of pupils clearly

branded as less able. One school experienced this problem acutely
in a two-band structure – academic and non-academic – and
found that Caribbean pupils in particular refused to accept the
non-academic label ('academic' here refers to those considered
capable of passing any examinations). This school also found the
de-streaming process hard to manage in conditions of unstable staffing. The question of ability grouping in schools (like
that of the question of selective or non-selective schooling) raises
wider issues of profound importance to the education service:
what is the relationship between schools and the labour market in
the short and long term? What proportion of 'failures' should be
tolerated – either defined as those leaving school from the lowest
stream, or those leaving without any relevant examination passes?

Integration, the theory and the practice

Both secondary head-teachers based many early policy
changes on an unwritten assumption: that individual immigrant
pupils would in effect 'become English', adopt the *mores* of the
school and the local English population, cease to consider themselves as members of groups which were 'different', and that this
one-sided process would in itself be a cure for bad race relations.
But in the course of their work both heads came to reject this
assumption; to feel that the formula 'we're all the same here' was
an inadequate basis for school policies, however generous the
impulse behind it might have been. It could not deal with black–
white hostility in school, nor could it deal with the real
difficulties of minority pupils. Instead, both heads were developing the idea that the school should accept and reflect both cultural differences and also the kind of group solidarity among
West Indian and Asian pupils which might arise because of their
status and experience in the local community – in other words,
because of race relations. In one case, this led to the special appointment of a community liaison worker already mentioned,
and also to reorganization of the non-teaching side of the school
to provide smaller units and more pupil participation in a house
system. In the other school, it underlay changes in the curriculum to give all pupils much more factual information about
race and other societies. This was provided in normal subjects,
and also in a carefully planned fourth-year social-studies course

taken by the whole year group. In both schools, racial and national groupings for activities were to be encouraged, rather than thwarted, when pupils wanted them.

The kind of curriculum changes outlined by Hugh Cunningham in chapter 8 are dealt with from a rather different perspective by Margaret Nandy in chapter 7. She argues that teaching about race relations should be part of more general social studies which should start at least as early as first-year secondary pupils. This should aim at the gradual development of the concepts needed for social analysis, and of the habit of making rational judgements. This would be a course aimed quite explicitly at reducing group hostility based on the difference of other groups.

At least one further major point emerges from all the contributions: the necessity for an overall school policy, for a consistent approach involving, if possible, all staff, and at least a number substantial enough to set the standard. This point is made strongly by Denis McCarthy in the first chapter and born out in many ways by the other writers. For example it would be admirable but of limited value if the head-teacher had a natural gift for communicating with difficult children but the rest of her staff did not see this as their role. It would not be much use introducing a broad-based curriculum, with a view to improving race relations in school, if the lowest stream of the school remained constantly and predominantly black. It would not be much of an advance to make a special appointment of a language teacher, or a community liaison worker, if the rest of the school then treats them as the 'immigrant' teacher and shrugs off responsibility. This overall school policy calls both for considerable administrative gifts in the head-teacher, and also for fairly stable staffing: high turnover and high illness rates must be cut down.

If the approaches described above are broadly accepted as worth trying, they begin to provide some standards for judging multi-racial schools and candidates for responsible posts in them. In a good school we should expect to find staff who were well informed about the diverse national groups served by the school, both as groups living in the locality, and as individual families; the whole staff would show and the school organization reflect a sophisticated concern with language; the activities of the school in the curriculum, and in extra-curricula activities, would reflect both the diverse origins of pupils, and an attempt to solve some of the many problems of race relations; finally, we should expect to see considerable thought, teaching effort and resources devoted to the most backward, least apparently promising pupils in the school. The points, again if we rely on the experience of the contributors to this book, are equally important at all age levels. Thus there is a range of attributes which infant, junior and secondary-school teachers should share in common.

This brings us to an issue which has so far been raised only indirectly: the question of teachers' attitudes. The book has focused on practical, to a large extent administrative, measures. It has hardly looked at teachers' attitudes – those unspoken or spoken assumptions about groups of pupils (West Indians, Pakistanis, Indian, English or Irish children from unskilled homes) which can have an all-important effect on the atmosphere of a school and the progress of the pupils. Had we asked the contributors to the book certain general questions about race and immigration, in the manner of an attitude survey, or had we asked them whether they believed the education system was broadly fair or unfair to working-class pupils, we should no doubt have obtained a considerable range of views, and a considerable range of feelings. What united them all was their lack of cynicism, their commitment to their own schools, a determination to make them work well and, above all, willingness to change existing routines to achieve this. It is not surprising that, in the event, the search for better methods often seems to have led to greater introspection among teachers, and in fact to have changed attitudes. But although attitude change is implicit in some of the teaching practices described, none of the writers deals directly with the subjective side of life in a multi-racial school. This area has in fact been very little explored in Britain, apart from an occasional and sometimes illuminating exposé of crude racial or class prejudice. As a gesture towards further exploration, we have included a short narrative bibliography which is particularly relevant to teachers' understanding of their relationship to pupils. The most striking point about attitudes which emerges explicitly and implicitly from the experience of the teachers writing for this book is that *fairness is not enough: it must be deepened with knowledge.*

One question which follows, and which is of special relevance to groups organizing training of any kind, is 'what kind of knowledge?' There can be as much bias and ill-will in an accumulation of facts as in perfect ignorance. Again turning back to the book, two kinds of knowledge have in practice been singled out by the writers: first, knowledge of individual families, their economic position and the emotional position of the child in the family; secondly, knowledge about the situation of those families as part of minority groups living in Britain – basically, the experience of being black in a white country, in its practical and psychological effects. Of course this must be seen in the wider context of the class position of English pupils. But acknowledging the wider context must not mean denying the facts about race relations. This appears to make considerable demands on the minds of teachers, for it really adds up to their identifying closely with their pupils, not only overcoming the barriers to communication, which we defined earlier as a main feature of multi-racial schools, but going one better – making an additional imaginative effort.

Whether the profession is attracting people capable of this; whether colleges are developing courses which will be of practical value in it; whether authorities are actively seeking teachers who will make the special effort and getting them into multi-racial schools – these are wide questions which we cannot answer. But if we look simply at the bare bones of the situation of multi-racial schools, it is clear that teachers are in a uniquely good position to be able to develop new insights and approaches. On the one hand they are sufficiently concerned with individuals to overcome the self-consciousness of inter-racial contacts; on the other hand they are in situations which are capable of being organized to promote communication between diverse groups. These advantages are much less true of neighbourhoods, or of workplaces. It may be that the experience of teachers in a well-organized multi-racial school may be able to withstand the generally punitive or squeamish approach of the majority towards minorities, which characterizes the world outside school. Perhaps it may also act as a stimulant to authorities and colleges to show more professional concern with multi-racial schools.

There is, however, one major limitation on this experience even in the best-run school, the fact that most of the black people whom a white teacher is in contact with are of lower status – within the school – than the teacher: they are children or parents. The great advantage of having a multi-racial *staff* is not only to provide black authority figures for the black pupils, but to provide a black peer-group for the white teachers. It would of course be important that the black teachers should not be prejudiced themselves against minority pupils, and also that there should be a 'school policy' of the kind we outlined above, and a general atmosphere in which staff talked to each other. But given these conditions, multi-racial staffing would be an enrichment. Authorities with many multi-racial schools should be pursuing a policy of active recruitment of black school-leavers into teaching.

We have looked in this book at some major problems and some important positive work in a handful of schools. Whether this work will be pushed further, and whether the kind of standards which it sets will become generally accepted, it is hard to judge. It is equally hard to judge the potential effect on the outside community of an increasing number of successful, lively and responsive multi-racial schools. They could be treated as show-pieces. They could, on the other hand, inspire other institutions in our society to exhibit a similar responsiveness to a mult-racial world.

The authors would like to state that any opinions expressed are their own and not that of their local education authority.

1 The Organization of a Multi-Racial Primary School

Denis McCarthy

I arrived as the head of a North London Junior and Infant school in February 1960. It was housed in a typical nineteenth-century, three-decker building, with high ceilings and windows, inadequate play space and surrounded by old houses and some pre-war flats. The corridors and stairs were narrow and ill-lit, and the work conditions in general made it very difficult for teachers even to attempt to provide a modern educational environment.

The total number of pupils, over the seven years I was there, rose from 320 to 450, covering the whole of the age range from five to eleven. At the same time the proportion of children of overseas parentage rose from 10 per cent to 57 per cent, most of them either Greek or Turkish Cypriots or West Indians, with smaller groups of Indians, Pakistanis, French Mauritians, Italians and West Africans. Almost all these children had come from overseas. At that stage there were very few British-born 'immigrant' pupils. Their arrival, particularly that of the West Indians, seemed to us to happen very suddenly.* It was a common occurrence at one period on a Monday morning to have a long queue of people outside my room who had just arrived in the country, or from another part of Britain. The classes rapidly filled up, and I opened four new ones in the course of about three years. I started with eight and finished with twelve.

The immigrant pupils seemed at first to mean nothing but

* West Indian migration had been going on throughout the 1950s, particularly since 1954, the annual figures closely following the demand for labour in Britain. Women were always well represented, and it was probable that couples would eventually call their children to join them – particularly after free movement of labour was ended by the 1962 Commonwealth Immigrants Act. For a full explanation of the migration from the Caribbean, India and Pakistan, see E. J. B. Rose and associates, *Colour and Citizenship*, Oxford University Press, 1969, Pt 2, chs. 6–8.

problems – problems which threatened to overwhelm the school. For one thing, the ordinary administrative tasks which are taken for granted in the running of a school – routines like the keeping of an accurate register, medical examinations and records, the collection of dinner money, even the serving of school meals – now required far more effort to carry out and sometimes could not be done at all. This was not only because of language and culture differences, but also because of the amount of moving which the immigrant families did – a subject to which I shall return later. In the second place, we were faced with a tremendous increase in discipline problems in the classroom and playground. Aggression, noise, destructive behaviour and disobedience increased. Boys would push, punch and kick other children, seize toys from them and, when corrected, would laugh in the teacher's face. Girls were restless and would talk, play or giggle during class or assembly. There is no shortage of explanations for this, some very familiar – the frustration of the physical conditions of the homes, mostly one room; broken or unhappy families. Some of the West Indian children also had emotional difficulties because of the piecemeal build-up of families in Britain. But two causes of dissension were new to the teachers. One was the strong sense of racial and national consciousness among the children. In our experience it was not true that young children are free from racial consciousness. Both immigrant and English children were influenced by their parents' views, and those near the top of the school took a lot of notice of outside events. We found that the older West Indian children became very colour conscious. At least once, a group in the dining-room declared 'no whites at this table'. Incidents which, to the teacher, seemed trivial, would be turned into questions of colour. We also found there was often rivalry and bad feeling between children from different West Indian islands, and that sometimes fairer skinned children would call darker ones 'black' in scathing tones. The Cypriots were often against the West Indians (one was once heard to say to a West Indian, 'go back to your own country'). Conscious efforts had to be made if children were not to group themselves along ethnic lines. The second cause of dissension which was new to teachers, was the language problem which quite simply prevented many of the children from understanding or taking part in the life of the school. Frustrated and bored, they had few productive outlets for their energies. Sometimes racial and language factors were hard to disentangle. The older children resented adult correction and authority and sometimes took it as a personal grudge. West Indian children in fourth-year junior classes who had difficulty in making themselves understood, no longer regarded it – as the younger ones did – as rather amusing. Once we began to tackle the language problem, and children started to make progress, the bad behaviour declined; children became less aggressive, more cooperative with other children and the teachers, although they might go in for a spate of noisy vocalizing as they tried out their new powers of communication. The other side of the coin was the problem of the withdrawn and silent child – easier for the teacher, perhaps, but a product of the same general circumstance as the aggressive one.

I now come to the third and major problem which we faced as a school, the educational one. I shall concentrate here on the junior age-group, where the problems were most difficult for the class teachers, and try to describe the situation from their point of view. They found themselves faced with a much wider range of ability than before – or range of handicap. In addition to the all-ability range of the previous unstreamed class, there was a very heavy 'tail-end' with all the various kinds of educational disability. If the school had been streamed by ability, most of the children from overseas would have been placed in the 'C' streams because of their inadequate English. But, of course, within this group of children with language difficulties there was a range of ability just as among the fully English-speaking. In the unstreamed class provision had to be made simultaneously for the English-speaking child with an extensive vocabulary who had the ability and desire to go ahead rapidly, the average, the maladjusted, the deprived and the backward child. In addition, there might be a non-English-speaking child of student parents, able to learn the language quickly, a child from a peasant background who was slow to learn it, and a child who spoke a variant of English but not the English his teacher required. Within one class were children who had just arrived in Britain, or from another part of the country, and children who had been right through infant school here. When our overseas pupils reached the top of the infant age-range, it sometimes seemed as if they had overcome their difficulties. By this time they had become fully accustomed to school life and could speak to and understand their friends and teachers. They could read, their use of apparatus for reading and mathematics had taken on real meaning, and they could participate in a wide range of activities with some satisfaction. But we found that there were also difficulties for children who had been right through infant school here and were quite familiar with both school and the locality. For example, a child wholly educated here, and able to communicate freely with his classmates, often had a superficial command of English, which might actually conceal serious gaps which would be revealed in his written work. Another problem, in our case mainly affecting the Cypriots, was that children would come to school tired and restless after attending Saturday or evening classes in their parents' language and culture. Understandable, since the parents are anxious that the child's links with their community shall not be lost but, nevertheless, many children found this too much for them to take in together with their school lessons. The standard of written work in some cases declined among juniors who had been educated entirely in Britain. But at least with them, the experienced teachers could ensure they had some understanding of the child's stage of development, and his educational background. This was much more difficult with the newcomers to the school — who formed a very high proportion of any class at any one point in time.

The assimilation of a young child from overseas into the life of an ordinary English school can be a very difficult experience for him indeed. The first experience of school for any child, even when he is well prepared and looking forward to it, can be bewildering, tiring and over-stimulating. How much more difficult it is for a child coming from a country of open spaces, hot sunshine, village life to one or two rooms in a house in a London street. He may not have been told what school is like, because his parents probably have no idea themselves, and on his arrival he finds he speaks a different language and/or is a different colour from his teachers and other children. At our school some children had never played, and were bewildered when placed in the new entrants' class where other children were playing with toys, sand, water, clay and paint. Those who came without *any* idea of what school would be like expected a programme of continuous formal work. New children would often stand for some days in the classroom just watching other children, listening to the strange sounds and words all round them, being spoken to by teachers and other children in a foreign language or a tongue different in some way. Similarly in the playground it was some time before they joined in, and the feeling of isolation was greater when both parents went out to work, and children not only stayed to dinner, but after school as well, in a play-centre.

Children of junior age faced the same strangeness as the very young children, but they were more mature and had clearer expectations of what school would be like. Many children showed that they were disoriented not just during the settling down period but for some time afterwards. Children who had been to school in their own country were puzzled by the kindly treatment they received from teachers, and the lack of rigid conformity. But in some cases, the children's expectations had not been formed overseas at all. They might have been to school in another part of London or of Britain, where immigrants were a small minority or where a child was the only coloured immigrant among many others. For these too, the arrival at our school meant considerable adjustment. The many new entrants meant we had a very large number of children to assess, and they were particularly hard to assess. How was a teacher to fit a child of ten with no understanding of English into a class of ten year olds? How could she find out about his ability? What could he do in class? In normal circumstances, records and standardized tests would give an indication of ability in the basic subjects, and non-verbal intelligence tests often help to diagnose the backward child. We found however that standardized tests were unusable for non-English-speaking children and of little use for most West Indian children, apart from the mental arithmetic tests. Even children with some knowledge of English found these tests incomprehensible. The non-verbal reasoning test we also found was often unsuitable because the explanation of examples that has to be given by the teacher could not be understood and the content of the pictures of diagrams were unfamiliar to overseas children.

We could have done more if we had built up a stable school population. One of the most aggravating problems was the number of immigrant pupils who *left*. If the children stayed in school long enough to move up through the junior classes, or better still if they had passed through the infants as well, it was possible to get a much better grasp of their difficulties and treat them accordingly. But all too often they did not stay. This was something which I discussed with the parents. Some of them used to go to great lengths to keep their children in the school – making a most impressive effort when you knew some of the awful journeys which this imposed on them. Some were willing to come a considerable distance on foot because they really wanted their children to remain in the school. But where they lived depended on where they were working, and where they could obtain the most reasonable accommodation, and, inevitably, the day came when they had to move too far away for the children to continue at our school.

What kind of work, then, could these children undertake, what kind of help could be given and how much, in a class of forty? Apart from the periods of time given to language work, reading, and the simple mechanical kind of arithmetic, how could these children be gainfully occupied when the rest of the class was engaged in ordinary school work? Most of them would want to paint and draw and take part in PE, but what about social-study lessons and follow-up work in group and individual work? When the class was producing individual or group books on some aspect of creative English, what work could these children do except straightforward copying or providing a pattern for the book? What stimulus could be provided? How long before frustration, particularly of the more intelligent ones, would cause disciplinary problems? Perhaps I should here include some examples of written work of children who were to some extent able to take part in class.

N. was an intelligent Greek Cypriot girl who had been with us eighteen months. She had arrived without any knowledge of English. She wrote:

In Cyprus the winters are warm. Sometimes when we have wind some people were 3 catigens. Atschool we been 8 o'clock with the coach we had a card with stamps in it and our father pou 3 each for a week we had a hall but we didn't sing or enything we doing in england. the morning we had to go that hall and dring our milk in the cup we had Greek bread. and we stay 15 mints out to play. And 3½ we had to go straight home out of the gate was a little ladie with a prum with sweet nothing cost 6d sweet the money was 3d.

N. in a few months after she wrote this had to start coping with secondary-school work. Another fourth-year child, M., a Greek Cypriot boy, wrote:

In Cyprus I had to go to school bout it ye had some hoir we will it hot by the mater in the school but if we have no hoir we not have the hot by the mater and we come home at 8 o'clock in the naght.

M. had been in school for fifteen months. A third-year West Indian boy F., who had been with us for three years wrote:

in my country i hard some animals and the animals horses, pigs crocodiles and cows. and it is sunshine and i boes go on my horses and the i does fight plenty and in my school there are children and a teacher. and the teacher was doing and the noowh and wher's all thele was it ald in a ahdt.

It would not be exaggerating to say that there were times when the teachers positively disliked some of their pupils, because faced with this situation, they felt guilt-ridden. They felt 'Here is a situation with which I cannot cope. Am I a failure? Or, if I'm not a failure, why aren't I doing so well?' There was a violent self-criticism: they weren't doing their job efficiently, they weren't getting the rapport they ought to after twenty years or ten years teaching. It was not, in my view, a question of prejudice, but rather 'Here children challenge me in a way I've never been challenged before. And I don't like it because I haven't got the skills, I haven't got the equipment in school, my classes are too large, I'm not getting extra help. What am I to do? Shall I give up teaching?' In the early stages some people retreated into their shells, and some became hostile – both quite normal reactions because the teachers were afraid of the situation. Yet, over the seven years we maintained an almost completely stable staff, and lost no teachers because of bad morale.

I come now to what we actually did. I would stress here that the approach of a particular school may be appropriate only to the circumstances of that school, but it seems to me that there is one important factor in any multi-racial situation. The attitude of all who work in these schools must be consistent, in sympathy with the many different needs of the children and, above all, relevant to the current situation rather than looking back on the school as it was. This attitude is not achieved merely by believing it should exist. There are several prerequisites: first and foremost – the relationship between the head and the class teachers. If the head's relationship with the staff is right then their relationships are right with their children, and therefore the relationship with the parents is right. If the head applies pressure from the top for standards, and is backward looking and critical of what the teachers are not doing, and the fact that the children can't do things that children in other schools can do, then the pressure is on and the children suffer because the pressure is on them too. Secondly, for the teachers, it is above all vital to have a realistic view of the work which the children can be expected to do, the work they are hoping to get from the children. But to achieve the right attitude one needs not only better understanding of the children, but also the rethinking of teaching methods and organization, practical assistance through additional teaching and non-teaching staff, and finally, more money.

The transition to teaching for an international, multi-racial school community was not an easy one for us. Teachers and ancillary workers who had been used to certain ways of working found that not only had the nature of their work changed but it had become more arduous, even exasperating. Standards of attainment and behaviour did not seem to match up to those that had been customary in the school five, ten or fifteen years earlier. This was a cause of resentment to longer-serving members of the school and could not be lightly brushed aside or ignored as if it did not exist. I felt that if a unified approach was to be developed it was essential that all those concerned with the children must feel they were receiving support and that their difficulties were recognized. The school as a whole must have the understanding, approval and financial support of the LEA.

We were allowed extra secretarial hours, which helped on the administrative side. We were also allocated more hours for women helpers, which was useful in dealing with the numerous social problems, but was also a boost to the morale of the helpers. They began to feel that there was a recognition of their difficulties and their personal contribution to the life of the school. They also had a contribution to make in many different ways in the activities of the classroom. This closer involvement gave them a more understanding, sympathetic attitude. The very nature of some aspects of their work led to a closer contact with parents which provided a background they had not had previously.

Parallel with these developments there were growing contacts between the school and the parents. Teachers tried to meet as many of the parents as they could and more seemed to be taking a greater interest in the work their children were doing. We provided as many opportunities as possible for parents to come into school and therefore to know more about its work. I made myself available to parents at any time during the day to discuss any matter of concern, however trivial it may have seemed. This provided many opportunities for correcting misunderstandings and discussing the difficulties of some children. Such contacts would not have been possible had parents been restricted by a system of appointments. But none of this, valuable though it was, affected our main task which was, after all, to teach.

Teaching methods and organization evolved as the situation changed, approaches were reconsidered as more staff became available. At the beginning teachers were receiving into their classes children with whom no contact could be made and who did little more than sit in the classroom and amuse themselves until the end of the day. Here, then, was a situation which had not been met before in quite the same circumstances, and both experienced and inexperienced members of staff were groping for ways of dealing with it. The two questions that urgently required answers were how can these children be taught and what can they be taught within the organization of a British primary school which is in no way regarded as a school for overseas children?

At first it seemed that this was another type of slow-learning problem which could possibly be dealt with in the same way as others had been before. The children, we thought, could be fitted into groups of backward readers and given a certain amount of follow-up work until the next group lesson. In the early stages this worked reasonably well, the part-time teachers taking out from each class any child requiring special help in reading. This included non-English-speaking children, those who had little English, the backward overseas children and backward British children. Some of the immigrant children made good progress and began to take a general interest in books both in the class and main libraries, but these were children educated in Britain, or children of white-collar or professional parents. The children without *any* knowledge of English, did not do nearly as well, and for the level at which they required attention there was no provision in the existing group work. Whereas some of the other children were returning to their classrooms each day at least able to 'hold on' to something, these non-English-speaking children had virtually nothing.

The steep rise in the number of immigrant children, accompanied by the high percentage turnover, made it essential to reconsider our approach. It is important to stress the point of a high percentage turnover as this was initially one of the most difficult matters that had to be faced. Not only was it disheartening for the teachers both full-time and part-time, but it hampered general class progress and the establishment of stable groups. It was clear that the non-English-speaking children would have to be given help of a kind different to that normally provided in the special groups.

So, the next step in the development of a different approach was the grouping of children who had no knowledge whatsoever of English. The groups were made up of ten children who were taken each day by a part-time teacher. An attempt was made to teach these children English by the direct method. Simple language patterns were developed by conversation based on a book containing bold pictures and short sentences. Simple games were played with the children and actions were mimed. The children enjoyed this and felt a sense of achievement in being able to get their tongues round new words and make themselves understood. The books that had been studied for the picture content became more interesting still to the children as the words were related to the pictures and they began to 'read'.

Although progress with the non-English-speaking children was being made and the pressure, to a small degree, was being taken off the class teacher, it was apparent that this additional help was not enough. In the first place, the amount of time which could be allocated to any group each day was inadequate and allowed for little more than that described. If a broader approach was to be made, it was clear that more time would be needed each day so that the scope of the activities could be widened, thus being of greater benefit to the child and the class teacher. It was also clear that, in any further developments of this work, the West Indian children would have to be included. The majority of immigrant children, ranging from the non-English speaking, through those with some knowledge of English, to the West Indian who speaks English, had one problem in common and that was little or no grasp of the patterns of standard English required by the educational activities in school.

Immigrant children up to this point had either received extra help in groups of backward children or had had group work in the direct method and then, if sufficient progress had been made, entered a backward readers' group. But when we examined the work of some of the children who had attended special groups for some time and were considered to possess a fair grasp of the language, it was quite disturbing to realize just how inadequate they were in language skills. The following is an example of a piece of writing to describe a picture painted by a Greek Cypriot boy who had been in the school for two and a half years and was nine years of age:

christmas plag and he sing ing in the christ mas play.

A West Indian child aged nine wrote:

one day, a man with a girl – they was ran in they stop, have you got any money 1 and 3d, thank you I will go and they a pack to eat, good dy.

Although we realized the limitation of the work it was, we felt, the best that could be attempted with our existing staff. Fortunately, however, in 1965, the Department of Education and Science permitted the recruitment of a limited number of 'off quota' teachers to assist schools in areas with a high immigrant population, and two teachers were allocated to the school. The first was not only experienced but had been engaged in language teaching and quickly grasped the depth and diversity of our particular problem. The second teacher, although inexperienced both generally and in language teaching, was anxious to learn the techniques of language teaching from her colleague and was sympathetic to the problems of immigrant children. It was now possible, with two full-time teachers and additional hours allocated for non-teaching staff, to reconsider our approach. The continued growth of the number of immigrant children of all ages made it necessary, as a first step, to survey afresh the extent of the problem.

Each immigrant child between the ages of five and eleven was seen separately by the language teacher to assess the degree and type of language disability. This proved a formidable task and took several weeks. The longest interviews were held with the West Indian children and those whose language was not English but had progressed well enough to make themselves understood and who could comprehend. Apart from children who had no English at all, the gaps in language background, the degree of comprehension and the lack of a pattern of language of the others was staggering.

The second step was a staff meeting to allow for a complete picture of the school problem to be given and suggestions to be considered. It was quite obvious that an extension of the existing organization, i.e. class teachers responsible for their classes and part-time teachers taking out groups each day from these classes, would be unsuitable because of the diverse needs of the children. Equally it was clear that it would be neither desirable nor practicable to have a reception class or classes for immigrant children. Neither was it a possibility to reduce the size of the classes to any extent sufficient to make an impact, for this would need far more than two 'off quota' teachers. It was decided to experiment with the idea of a language centre which would be as flexible as possible in order to meet the constantly changing situation of our school.

The difficulty of suitable accommodation was overcome by dual use of the junior library and an adjoining room which had been used as a storage room for visual aids. The library remained available for small groups of children and individuals for work and reference during lesson time, in addition to being in use at break times and lunch times. The language centre, manned by the two full-time teachers and assisted by a non-teaching member of staff, was to be in no way separate from the rest of the school.

The essence of the whole experiment was cooperation between the class teachers and the centre. In school the 'home' of each immigrant child was his own classroom and the progress he made would, in part, be due to the effective following up of work by his class teacher.

The large number of children requiring extra help made it essential for an order of priority to be made. The children chosen were those who had no knowledge of English at all, children whose language severely hampered their work and those West Indian children who had great difficulty in verbal communication and almost no correct language pattern in standard English. In all, about half the immigrant pupils attended in groups of about twenty-four. This number could be exceeded on occasion if, in the opinion of the centre teachers, the types of activity at that particular time were suitable. If we had had more resources we might have given this help to 75 or 80 per cent. The attendance of children throughout the day was planned in advance by discussion with class teachers. The idea was to send them to the language centre during the periods in the day when they could not participate actively in ordinary lessons. This criterion gave considerable flexibility to the arrangement and permitted children to stay in the centre for quite long periods and return later in the day if thought desirable. In this way many children during the course of the day could be given considerable special attention.

The flexibility of the scheme and the variety of the work made it possible to accommodate on arrival any new child admitted to school who urgently required individual help. It also allowed for the return to full classroom attendance of those judged able to fit in, and thus provided opportunities for those whose priority was lower to take their places. We felt it was more urgent for middle and upper juniors to receive as much help as possible and therefore fewer infant than junior children attended at first. These excluded infant children, however, received individual attention each day with conversation, pre-reading and reading activities from a part-time teacher.

Two things that soon became obvious were the rate at which consumable stock was being used, and the deficiency, both in quantity and kind, of suitable apparatus and material for the teaching of English as a second language. Initially, the language centre drew heavily on the school's stock of consumable items, borrowing pieces of apparatus in reading and number that could be spared from the infant classes, using the tape recorder and making all kinds of apparatus connected with language. Grants from the LEA helped to buy further consumable items, apparatus and books which made the organization of work a little easier and later on, tape recorders with headsets and simple teaching machines.

Although the commercially produced materials proved valuable in oral work and in individual activities, the most valuable contribution was the material made by the two teachers. The main criticism of many of the simple books considered suitable for language teaching overseas was the lack of appeal of the contents to overseas children or to the age range. Those for English children contained too much complex language.

The language centre presented a picture of a free and fluid situation where children could come and go for varying periods of time during the day and where they might take part in many different aspects of language work. Here, at one and the same time, might be seen a group discussion, individual apparatus work, conversation practice, modelling, painting, acting and reading. At the beginning of this new approach not all members of staff were in favour of it, partly because of the movement of children in and out of the classroom at different times during the day, and partly because of a feeling that teachers outside the normal staff structure were assuming responsibility for a school problem. As the beneficial effects, both on the immigrant children themselves and on the class organization, began to be felt, the new members of staff were readily accepted. Cooperation and understanding of their work increased and this was helped by their readiness to take part in all branches of school activity both during and after school hours.

The two teachers, aided by a non-teaching member of staff, developed their work as a team which in time widened its horizons. Dialogues about the home and school situations, which had formed the basis of the language work, now broadened out to take in a study of the neighbourhood. Shops, post office, railway station and parks were visited giving rise to varied opportunities for language work and development. An attempt was made also to help those children, particularly at the top end of the school, who, although they had made good progress and could fit more easily into a class, found work such as social studies very difficult. The vocabularly was so often outside their experience that they needed special preparation if they were to participate in the work of the class as an individual or as part of a group project. In the language centre this help was given by discussion, pictures, drawing and writing. After such preparation the children were at least able to participate more intelligently in the work of the class. In other words, we had got away from the rigid and rather artificial distinction between English speaking and non-English speaking and were able – within the limits of resources – to teach English according to the very different needs and stages of development of each individual.

What effect did all these changes have on the teachers? At first there had been a feeling of shock at the numerous difficulties and a concern for standards. Certainly at one point there was resentment; an older teacher remarked 'Why should they (the immigrants) have all this extra attention?' On the other hand many older teachers had throughout their careers faced seemingly insurmountable difficulties and had the resilience to put things in perspective, adjust their expectations and meet the new situation. Younger members of staff, although less experienced, displayed courage, initiative and imagination in their approach. Nevertheless, all the teachers found teaching a great strain. Young and old found they were much more tired at the end of the day than they used to be. It was also noticeable that there was a greater amount of absence through sickness. But sickness was not used as a means of avoiding difficulties, on the contrary, many teachers who were really quite unfit came to school to avoid makeshift arrangements being made for their children. A new spirit was developing in the school, a new attitude, an awareness of the different contribution that a teacher makes in a multi-racial school, was growing. Many passed through the stages of a feeling of shock at the sheer toughness of their task and the apparent lack of results, bewilderment as to the best method of dealing with the class situation and extreme physical tiredness. Nevertheless they came to terms with the task, accepted it as a challenge to their abilities as teachers, worked willingly and well and sought ways of making their teaching more effective.

How were the English parents affected, what were their attitudes? In general it would be true to say that most parents were tolerant and reasonable, but one became conscious of the fact that there was increasing concern over the number of immigrant children. There was a tendency for complaints and difficulties to be magnified when overseas children were involved, and more parents began to seek transfers to schools with a lower percentage of immigrants. It should be remembered, of course, that parents usually became more anxious about their children's progress as they moved up through the junior classes. The presence of immigrant children focused parental anxiety. It seemed, however, that the higher proportion of *coloured* immigrants caused greater parental disquiet than the total number of immigrants. Perhaps it was coincidental, but increased parental concern was paralleled by greater press, radio and television coverage of racial problems. Nevertheless, behind the racial feelings, the basic fear of the parent was that overseas children have learning difficulties and will thus absorb all the teachers' attention. They reason that in a class of forty children this is inevitable and the consequence is a neglect of their children and lower standards of attainment. This is a reasonable assumption which if allowed to remain unchallenged will result in a rapid deterioration of morale by parents, teachers and children.

The key to the problem is communication and good personal relationships. Parents need to be acquainted with some of the changes that have taken place in primary education. Their personal recollection of primary schools will be associated with memories of a rigid class structure, sets of textbooks for the whole class, irrespective of suitability for all, and learning at one level. The all important point to establish is that forty children with a very wide range of ability are not taught as a class, neither is one section of the class taught whilst others are sacrificed. It is necessary that parents really understand how grouping, and the use of additional full-time and part-time staff, improves the pupil–teacher ratio.

In our case, parents began to appreciate the provision we tried to make for all the children in the school. One part-time teacher ran special classes to extend and develop the *most able* children in the upper junior school. These children undertook extensive research projects visiting museums and other places of interest. Their work in mathematics was pursued in greater depth than would have been possible without the small-group, individual attention this teacher provided. Other part-time teachers gave help to those backward in reading and number work in small, tutorial-type groups.

All this in addition to the language-centre staff. Also – to move entirely away from the basic education side – we provided a visiting teacher to give violin lessons and another for cello lessons.

We found ways of making educational experiences relevant to most of our children despite their diversity of needs. Corporate activities by the whole school, throughout the age range, were frequent; the building up of a school orchestra, and at least one term each year devoted to a school project in which everyone cooperated, became school traditions. When this culminated in the making of films as part of the project, curriculum horizons were further extended.

In any discussion of the present standards of the school two points need to be considered: firstly, standards have changed, which is not another way of saying they have dropped; the content of primary education has broadened out, the narrow measuring instruments of mechanical testing are inappropriate for much of the work: secondly, the neighbourhood has changed over the years; a cross-section of the occupations is likely to present a less skilled pattern than in earlier years. Work achieved in any school is governed in part by the types of children and the range of their intelligence.

From my own experience of seven years in a multi-racial school it seems to me that attitudes are of paramount importance. If the attitudes of the teaching and non-teaching staff are balanced ones, then good personal relationships will develop between teachers and pupils and teachers and parents. Out of this will grow understanding, confidence and trust. But to develop these attitudes there must be an appreciation of what the school is in this changed situation. The very nature of a multi-racial school changes the emphasis of the work of its adult members –

much of it is social. If this fact is ignored frustration and resentment will follow.

We believe that the school can, and should, make a different kind of contribution in the community. Where teachers have faced up to the realities and have looked forward rather than backwards, then the extra contribution of the school can create an oasis of stability in the insecurity of a new multi-racial community.

2 Contact with Parents

Winifred Bindley

Introduction

I suppose anyone approaching our school will first be daunted by the building and its surroundings, so I will begin there. Ours is a four-storey building, opened under the School Board for London in 1889. I suppose in some ways it might even now be considered quite handsome as a building, but as a primary school it hardly qualifies. There are two schools housed here, our Infants school of about 350 children, and a Junior Mixed school of about the same size, but growing all the time. The building was designed for 'Boys, Girls and Infants', as the signs over the gates still show. This means that since boys and girls were presumably never supposed to meet, entrances and staircases are designed to make it as difficult as possible for the various floors to communicate. The lavatories are, of course well away from the school on the far side of the playground, washing facilities are few and at times Dickensian. We use the whole of the ground and four rooms on the first floor, and one of the four halls.

There are some advantages in the old building, however. For one thing these classrooms were designed for larger classes than we have, even if they were sitting in tiered rows. They are larger than most of the rooms found in modern buildings. There is no skimping on space in the corridors, either; they may be dark, but they are spacious. Somehow it is always possible to find an odd corner to take a small group of children, even if it is in the stock-room or a cloakroom.

The building is due to be completely remodelled very shortly, and will then have even more space, as covered outside play areas are built, and use is made of the very high rooms and corridors by inserting mezzanine floors. Then, too, we shall have an infant playground, and shall no longer have to share with the junior girls and their netball pitch. To be fair, we should have had this long ago, but the extra ground was occupied by a five-storey police station, built during the First World War, and only vacated within the last year.

If the outside of the building is rather forbidding, I doubt if it looks all that different to the children than other buildings in their neighbourhood. If they have been born and brought up in Islington, the chances are that their horizons are limited to terraces of ugly little nineteenth-century houses, church halls, interspersed with small factories, garages and workshops. School, bounded on one side by the Gas Board and on the other by the Victorian frontage of the municipal baths, is just a larger, more spacious version of home.

From the streets of little houses, then, come most of our children. About 60 per cent of their parents came from overseas, and have memories of warm Cypriot beaches and mountains, or of open-air life in the Caribbean. Nowadays, most of the children we take into school were born in London, but their parents have not experienced any sort of school in this country, not even, as the English parents have, the more formal schools of twenty to thirty years ago. The children (at least the first from any family) come to school totally unprepared for what they will find there, and are either bewildered or over-excited by the freedom they are offered. I suppose we could decide to run a more formal school, and indeed we often have to be more directive and formal towards a child for his first few weeks but we believe that the methods we use will in the end be the most valuable for these children.

Because of this lack of a common background among our children and their parents, we have made special efforts to contact parents, to explain to them just what we are aiming to do in school, and to listen to them when they express their hopes and aims for their own children. Our English parents find it difficult enough to understand the enormous changes in methods that have come about in modern primary schools since they were schoolchildren themselves; but for our immigrant parents the sight of small children moving about at will, and doing nothing but 'play' is absolutely astonishing.

Obviously we had to get together with the parents, try to meet their expectations without compromising our own ideas, try to explain to them what we are trying to do for their children, above all to get them to come and see that despite the apparent chaos of children moving freely around, a good deal of learning was going on all the time. I don't think we have really succeeded yet, but we have taken a few halting steps along the way, and with every step forward the task becomes easier. Our approach to parents is also guided by another feeling altogether. We are only too well aware of the bad feeling and discrimination that can be found in our area.

There seemed to be no focus for the population around the school, no place where the people could come together for a common purpose, perhaps to solve some of the problems which they in fact shared in common. Any attempt to make ours into a 'community school' presupposed that there would be a community around us to start with. This is patently not so, there are only a few families in the school who have been living in the area more than ten years, most of our children were not born in the borough. Nearly all our parents see their present home as a temporary one, just until something better turns up. So, on the whole, the population not only feels itself to be temporary, it is likely to be just passing through. One of our difficulties in school is a 30 to 40 per cent turnover. But it can be a very lonely existence for anyone living in such an area. Perhaps there was something the school could do? It seemed to us that the school could at least provide a place for people of different races and creeds and languages to meet, where they would all have in common their interest in their children. Perhaps, too, the school could help to relieve some of the loneliness and isolation felt by newcomers to the district. Getting people together may be a laudable activity, but unless they come together for a purpose, it is hardly likely to succeed. So we set out to find purposes that could serve to bring people together, that might eventually build a community around our school where only individual families were before. If at the same time we could also begin to reach some understanding with our parents about the aims and methods of the school, then this would be an added bonus. I don't know how many years it will take to make ours a community school, or whether this will ever be possible until the local population is rehoused and more settled. All the staff of the school felt that it was worth trying, that it was worth considerable effort on our part and, however little we succeed, we shall surely have done something.

Having decided on a definite policy of contact with parents with the two aims of parent–school and parent–parent understanding in mind, we took a good look at our chances. We had heard of, some of us had worked in, schools where the parents were so cooperative they almost took over. It didn't seem likely that this could happen to us. But we had the advantage that we were an infant school, that small children cannot bring themselves to school and register their names, that at least one grown-up must come with them. (There is only one child in the school whose parents we have never seen, an older sister brought him on the first day, with a label round his neck!) Mostly, our contact would be with the mothers, because both in our own and in the societies from which immigrant families came, mother is traditionally responsible for the small children. But we knew, too, that most of the mothers went out to work, or would start to as soon as their child began school. There are all sorts of different ideas about working mothers, some condemnatory, some guiltily explanatory. But in our area we knew why they worked. They had to. Over one third of our children come from families poor enough to qualify for free dinners. Lots of our mothers are bringing up their families on their own. Even where the father is earning a reasonable wage, there is no hope of a better house in an area with a little grass and a few trees unless the mother goes to work too. This might point to evening activities for parents, but there were the staff to consider too. Any teacher who puts everything into a day's teaching cannot and should not be asked to return to school too often in the evenings less she become stale and tired, and the children suffer as a result. So we settled for a mixture of day and evening and weekend activities, and as the educational year progresses there are fewer out-of-school events to tax the energies of a tiring staff.

Some of the things we tried were obviously successful, others were apparent failures, but at least we are making an effort, and it does seem that the parents are grateful for the efforts we make. There is a warm and friendly atmosphere in the school, and it is quite obvious that parents feel free to come in and out as they please. We have noticed with some satisfaction the changing situation in the corridors before and after school. When we first opened the doors and said to parents 'Come in' two and a half years ago, they came in on rainy days to wait for their children, and we could have drawn a chalk line down the corridor, and marked it 'Whites' on one side and 'Blacks' on the other. And although they all responded to a 'good afternoon' from me, they hardly ever spoke to each other. Now the hubbub in the corridors, both before and after school, is busy, parents of all races are found chatting together, some of them come early especially to meet their friends, and I often stop at 10.15 to join a still chatting group before they leave to go home and sleep after their night's work.

First contacts

The first time we meet the families of the children we are to teach is usually when they come to register their child for school. For us this is a vital meeting, and all our future relationships with the child and his parents may depend on the impression they have of the school this first time. The office is so arranged that there is never a desk between the headteacher and her visitor. It is a tiny office, shared by the school secretary and the deputy head, and there are always interruptions from children coming with messages, or to show me good work, or just to tell about a new baby or a chance of a new house. For the parent who does not speak English, or one used to a more formal relationship between children and teachers, it must be very confusing. I think the fact that the children feel so free to come to me at any time, and that I am always ready to find time to take an interest in them, shows that we care for human relationships in the school. The children, accustomed to seeing many visitors about the school, speak to the waiting parent, or to the child who is the cause of the visit.

It isn't always easy to get all the information we need about a child. Parents from overseas can usually produce a passport or a birth certificate, some of them thoughtfully bring an old envelope with their address. For others we sometimes seek the help of a juvenile interpreter, age about six, or resort to gestures. Often their lack of English makes my visitors seem abrupt and demanding. I used to find myself bridling slightly as they demanded 'My child five, you take.' But listening to myself on holiday abroad, struggling with an unfamiliar language, I realized how demanding I sounded, how my lack of vocabulary made me speak half-formed sentences that sounded rude. Now I have learnt to react with understanding to their brave attempts to speak English. Nevertheless, it can often take a long time to elicit the basic information.

I am embarrassed by the necessity to discover the country of origin of the parent, especially when the child was born in England. So that I can later fill in the forms that provide us with statistics, I must ask 'When did you come to England?' I have had parents reply defensively 'He's English, he was born here', but still I must persist 'Yes of course, but when did YOU come?' Then perhaps I can guess from where. The obviously Greek name comes from Cyprus, other names might be Maltese or Italian, and here we might talk of the countryside around their home, or the beautiful weather in Sicily. African names are more difficult, but I have learnt to distinguish between Nigerian (generally Ibo) names and 'the rest'. Names from the West Indies tend to be almost aggressively British, and I am beginning to recognize the different accents of the different islands. This amuses the parents who seem delighted that I should bother to ask which island. Most of the West Indians seem glad to find that I think it matters. And of course it does matter, because despite some common background culture, ideas and attitudes in St Lucia are different from those of, say, Jamaica; as different as those in the Highlands of Scotland might be from those in London.

So, after some time, and a lot of questions, we have established some sort of friendly relationship. I can feel my visitor warming to me, becoming aware that I am interested in his (or more usually her) child and his family. Then I have to upset everyone by saying 'I'm afraid it is very unlikely that I can take him into school until after he is five.' They have already heard from neighbours that we have a nursery class, that there are children of three and a half in the school. In the case of coloured parents, I can almost see their defences prepared for another racial rebuff. I explain carefully, I have a waiting list of 200, I only have room for thirty children in the nursery, there is nothing I can do. They don't really believe me, they point out that the child is lonely, or that his mother must go to work, that the family lives in one room, that he will learn English quicker in the nursery 'it will be better for the teachers then'. I show them the list, all the children with red stars because their mothers must work, they live in one room, or they do not speak English ... and nearly every child has a red star. I suggest that they might register the baby they have brought with them, 'perhaps he might reach the top of the list by the time he is four'. We laugh over this, but register him all the same. I try to help by suggesting other forms of help, but these are so few and far between in our area, and there is nearly always a long waiting list. There are two day-nurseries, open only to children with very urgent needs, that is, the children of unsupported mothers who must go out to work, or of mothers who are invalids. They are provided by the health authorities, who charge a daily fee, according to the means of the family. There are two other local-authority nursery classes and one nursery school, all part-time, and all with the usual long waiting lists. There is a voluntary nursery school which does excellent work with very small funds, relying on voluntary contributions and the annual sale of work to keep going. One of the local welfare clinics runs a playgroup, which children may attend three afternoons a week, and there is another playgroup run in a local hall four afternoons a week, which the school has tried to help. Under the urban development scheme, a new nursery class is being built, but however welcome, this can hardly make much difference to our ever growing waiting lists. Occasionally, I have the name of a registered baby-minder who has a vacancy, mostly there is nothing I can do. I know just how badly these children need some sort of nursery education. Most of them live in small rooms or flats, on busy roads, with no space to play indoors, and no hope of outdoor play. Most of their parents need to work, if there is ever to be any hope of improvement in the family's living conditions. For the most part grandmother, who 'at home' would have been looking after the children until they went to school, is still 'at home', and any aunties who are in England need to find a more remunerative job than looking after children. So I have failed these parents when I tell them I cannot offer their child a nursery education. Yet they don't seem to feel it is my fault, perhaps my use of that familiar term 'THEY' has helped to put them on my side, ' "THEY" won't let me take more than thirty under-fives at a time' but many parents have said 'I can see how difficult it is for you', and some even seem to feel sorry for me because I cannot take in all the children I would like to. But at least we have established contact, next time they will know their way into the school, into the office, and we can joke over my terrible memory for names.

Open days and 'shows'

Some of our most popular activities involving parents are the various 'shows' and special festivals we put on. Educationally, I am not sure that there is a great deal of value in small children putting on a polished performance for an audience. Most of the valuable work they do in music and drama comes spontaneously during ordinary lessons. But there is no doubt that there is a special thrill for parents in seeing their own child on a platform, performing. And if there is no particular value for the children, at least there is no particular harm, and they do get some enjoyment out of performing for their parents.

Our shows vary considerably in style and content, some being very ambitious, some very simple. We have the usual festivals, at harvest time and for Christmas. But we are luckier than many schools, because we can draw on songs and music from all over the world, and at harvest time we have sweet potatoes, green bananas and delicious little Greek nuts as well as the usual apples and packets of sugar. Parents are always invited to join us at these festivals, and we always word the invitation to 'all parents and friends', and add that small children are welcome. Sometimes the babies are noisy, or the toddlers chatter at the wrong moment, but these are festivals arranged for children, so we do not worry. At Christmas, we partly black out the hall, and sing our carols by candlelight. This is one occasion when we do not ask the children to perform, but the teachers and other friends of the school read the lessons and lead the prayers.

Other open days usually consist of having the school working normally for part of the time, when distinguished visitors like to visit the children in their classrooms. Most of the parents who come have seen the classrooms many times before, and are far more interested in the concert we put on in the hall. This may consist of a collection of items performed by each class in turn, or it may also have some extra plays or songs by a selection of the older children. We have found that many of our parents take time off work to come and see their children, and they often take the opportunity to talk to me, or to their child's teacher afterwards. For many of them, it is easier to come to the school after they have had a specific invitation than to come in and ask about something that is worrying them at any other time.

On a lesser scale, we have 'Family Prayers' every Friday morning at 9.30 a.m. Each week, a class takes it in turn to take Family Prayers, with the children choosing the hymns, saying their own prayers, and later the whole class performs its 'party piece' ... which may be a dramatized story, or a song or a poem, or perhaps showing and explaining a collection of pictures they have made. We remind parents of our Friday morning prayers every time we send out a circular letter, and although we rarely have more than twenty or so mothers, fathers and toddlers present, they are not always the same ones, and many parents make a special effort to attend when their own child's class is taking prayers. Again, this often provides the opportunity for parents to discuss their worries with a teacher.

A class for parents

Our building is also the headquarters of a thriving adult institute, with which we maintain very friendly relations. One day when discussing the proportion of immigrant children in the school, at that time about 57 per cent, with the principal, I was disappointed to learn that apart from the *au pair* girls in his English classes, the proportion in the institute was very low indeed. Surely there must be many of our parents who would enjoy some sort of class in the evening? Here, right on their doorstep, they were offered everything from car maintenance to embroidery, pottery to guitar playing. There was already in existence a class in dressmaking run specially for the teaching staff one dinner hour a week. When I discussed the problem with the staff, they came up with a suggestion. Why not a teacher–parent class, taking place after school? Most of the staff attending the class were absolute beginners in dressmaking, many of our parents are quite expert already. Perhaps a class where the parents would shine would help to topple teachers from that artificial pedestal where so many parents place them. The class was advertised, and so far we have only a few parents, but it is a good mixed group and the star needlewomen are all parents. Their children of all ages stay in school after everyone else has gone, and I run a Wednesday Club for them. We look at television sometimes, but mostly we play on the big toys in the nursery or play football in the playground, or sit and talk over orange juice and biscuits. I have got to know a number of families of children (ages from two to nine years) very well as families, and their mothers have learnt that teachers are human, not necessarily good at everything, and quite good company too. Not only that, but these same mothers are proving to be useful ambassadors for us as well. There was a long discussion about discipline at one sewing class, the mothers arguing for more of it, the teachers arguing that they were trying to teach the children to think for themselves, that if children heard nothing but a nagging teacher all day, they stopped listening to anything she said. (I don't think there was much dressmaking done that afternoon!) One of the mothers was heard propounding the teachers' point of view to her friends in the corridor the next morning. It was one of the dressmaking mothers too, who responded willingly to my invitation to come and talk to a large group of teachers at a conference called 'From the Caribbean', and told them just how she had felt about British schools, and British educational methods when she first met them. Another small success, this class, with the seeds of more things to come in it. And I notice that these are not the same parents who come on class outings, or come regularly to family prayers.

Outings

One of the ways we have found most successful in involving parents in the life of the school is through outings. As part of our educational activities we take a class of children out every week. This began with visits to the zoo in lieu of prize day, and has developed into a regular year-round activity. Last year we visited museums and the zoo in half-day trips. This year we are being a little more ambitious, and every week a class goes off on a ten-mile coach trip to the grounds of a college of education. There they can see acres of open space, trees, woods, lakes, a farm and all the things they see pictures of in books, that most of them have never seen before.

On my first exploratory visit to the zoo with five children, I was distressed by the sight of harassed children and teachers in long crocodiles being counted through every gate and door. One school had solved their problem by having each child hold on to a long piece of string! Meanwhile, I and my five children were enjoying ourselves. We had time to talk, and time to listen to each other. It was a pleasant family party. So we decided that for our class outings, we would aim at never more than five or six children per adult. And of course the first people we turned to were our parents. We were surprised at the result. There have never been more than five children per adult, often less; mothers and fathers, uncles and aunts have joined our outings. Sometimes they take a day off work to come, sometimes they have carted one or two toddlers around as well, and survived full of energy at the end of the day. One West Indian mother went to the Science Museum five times last year, and the zoo four times. Only the imminent arrival of twins has prevented her from joining our trips to the country! The outings, instead of being something dreaded by teachers, are something to look forward to, and we get a great deal of joy from the pleasure it brings to the parents as well as to the children. Those of us who were born and brought up in London used to be surprised to find that many of our children living only two and a half miles from the London Zoo had never been there. But most of our immigrant families had no tradition of family outings, and many of the rest found the business of organizing such a trip with four or five children, push-chairs, and the ever-rising cost of fares more than they could cope with. We were offering free travel and free entrance fees to parents who came to help. (We normally ask for a voluntary donation of 30p per child from the school children and about half of them do contribute.)

Our educational outings have led to a further activity. Travelling round the outer circle in Regent's Park on our way to a museum, I heard one little boy ask the 'Mum' sitting next to him

'Is that the sea?' She looked out at the boats on the lake, and at the footballers in the field beyond. 'Er, yes, dear, I expect so' she said. Later I talked to her. She had come from Barbados eight years before. Of course she had known the sea there, but since arriving at London Airport she hadn't seen the sea. She had heard that in England the sea was grey and cold, and probably looked very like the lake in the park. Would she like to see the sea again! Yes of course, but it was very expensive to get there.

A few weeks later I sent out a letter to parents, asking how many would be interested in a family outing to the sea on a Saturday in July. I can hardly say that the response was overwhelming, but it was sufficiently encouraging for us to commit ourselves to paying for threee coaches. I had not allowed for the well-known reluctance of our parents to answer any letters or fill in any forms! In the end when it was too late to order any more coaches we had a waiting list for vacancies of fifty. We made the trip as cheap as we could, with a reduced price for children, reducing still further for each successive child. The fifth child and over went free. Some staff were going, and volunteered to take a few children unaccompanied by their parents, but for the most part we stipulated families. We had fathers and mothers and children ranging from sixteen years old to a few months. We warned them to bring their own lunch, or be prepared to buy it in Clacton. We reminded them to bring swimming costumes and towels. We stocked the coaches with plastic bags and saw-dust (just in case!). The Saturday morning was fine and sunny, our ever helpful school-keeper opened the gate for us, and we gathered in the playground. The English families were in duffle coats and slacks, carrying their buckets and spades; most of the overseas families, including the Irish, were beautifully dressed, in their Sunday best, sister matching sister, and daughter matching mother. Little boys looked magnificent, and surprisingly subdued, in long-trousered suits. Our Australian teachers arrived in trousers, saying 'We want to see how the British behave on the beach! In Australia all the English wear long trousers, they do look silly.' We said nothing, just piled into the coaches, packed push-chairs and extra baskets in the back and set off.

Arriving at the coach park, we gave every family strict instructions about when and where to meet the coach for the return journey, and set off for the beach. One or two of the more experienced British families set off on their own, but most of the party stayed together, and remained as a party on the beach. One of the staff took a film of that day by the sea, and had the greatest difficulty in getting anything at all, since most families didn't seem at all sure what they should do, or how to behave in this unfamiliar situation. They sat on the beach, watching the teachers, and carefully following their lead. If you've never been on an English beach before, how are you to know what are the accepted ways of undressing and changing, how could you guess that it is possible to manage quite well, hiding beneath a towel? Most of the adults contented themselves with paddling, but the children all bathed, despite the coldness of the North Sea, and seemed tough enough to enjoy themselves.

Most of the families followed the teachers on to the pier in the afternoon, the children had rides in the miniature train, and everyone enjoyed candy-floss. Slot machines appealed to some of the parents, who lost a small fortune in pennies. On the way home they sang songs in the coach. The Australians said 'Now we know why the British wear so many clothes on the beach, they need them!' The West Indians and Cypriots talked nostalgically of the warm beaches and the warm sea 'at home'. The children suddenly made sense of all those pictures in their library books of children building sandcastles. Somehow a whole lot of different people from all over the world, of all ages, interests and experiences had joined together for fun, and for that day at least had become a community in the best sense of the word.

We could not stop there, of course. Our next family outing was a Christmas visit to the Ice Show, when 150 parents shared a half-day trip by coach to see Humpty Dumpty on Ice. Again we found that the shared experience and the shared enjoyment has helped people to come together, has begun to break down some of the traditional British reserve, and some of the hesitation of many overseas families to approach others. For example, two families, one Irish, one West Indian, have been living only a few doors away from each other for two years without meeting. As a result of meeting on the family outing last summer, they are now helping each other with redecorating their homes and with baby-sitting for each others' children. Obviously, we must go on providing this opportunity, and anyway, since we do not have to be responsible for large quantities of children, the staff enjoy the outings as much as anyone else. We are already planning the next seaside trip, and there have already been inquiries about when we shall start collecting for it.

Parents' evenings

Like most schools, we have the occasional evening meeting for parents. We have tried various ways of organizing these, some have been much more successful than others. All the staff asked for an opportunity to meet the parents during the first term of the educational year, and preferably without children in tow. We have tried two ways of doing this, one was a great success, the other an almost complete failure. The successful method was to invite the parents of only three or four classes at a time (We have nine infant and one nursery class) and to offer a playgroup for the children in the nursery, while the parents visited the classrooms and talked with the teachers. Most of the parents came with their children, and since we opened the school from 6.30 to 8.30 p.m., we found that they spaced themselves out nicely, and each teacher was able to give enough time to the parents who came. I was available in the library with cups of coffee and biscuits, and was able to chat in general terms with many parents, and tell them about the proposed re-modelling of the school, and what it would mean for their children. On these evenings, we were surprised to find that over half the families in the school were represented, and often by both parents. It was really valuable for the staff to meet so many of the fathers, and the parents were also pleased to be able to discuss their worries with the teacher at a time when she could listen to them, and didn't have to keep an eye on her class at the same time.

The following year, there seemed to be no reason why we should not repeat the success of the last series of meetings. However, we decided that all classes should have their evening meeting on the same day, and although we did not explicitly exclude them, we did not offer any special facilities for children. The result was a dismal failure, only fifteen families turned up, and although they showed considerable interest in new developments in the school, they were all families we had known for some time.

Obviously, the playgroup is a necessity, if we are to see any number of parents at our open evenings.

Other evening meetings we have tried are meetings on a specific subject. The most successful of these was a meeting on the teaching of reading. On a snowy night in January, eighty parents came to discuss this important topic. We started with an exhibition of books and materials used in the school for teaching reading, with teachers in attendance to explain how the apparatus was used. Obviously, our parents had great difficulty in seeing how matching two pictures had anything to do with learning to read. As the parents arrived in the Library for the meeting we handed them a 'Fun Quiz', assuring them that we weren't going to collect the papers afterwards . . . so no one would know their scores.

When everyone was gathered, we simply went through the quiz questions trying to explain how the questions were relevant to teaching reading. Some of the parents found it very difficult to understand why we no longer taught children the alphabet before they learnt to read. The meeting became quite hilarious as one or two West Indian mothers stoutly supported the methods by which they were taught. 'I learnt the alphabet, I learned THE, the, when I ask Patrick "What THE say!" he don't know.' 'But he can read the word when he sees it?', we asked. Yes, apparently he could. We explained the point about English not being a phonetic language, and one Nigerian father told us how true this was, and how difficult it had been for him to learn to read and write in English. The last question on the quiz asked if the parents themselves enjoyed reading. The same West Indian mothers who had been so critical of our methods both answered 'No, of course not.' They were answered by a Ghanaian mother who said, 'Well, then, you just let these teachers try it their way, and perhaps your children will be better readers.'

The really interesting thing about this meeting was the way all the parents became involved in the discussion, and the way they went on talking about reading for weeks afterwards. We may not have persuaded them all that we were going about the teaching of reading in the right way, but at least they seemed prepared to let us have a chance. Perhaps it helped that we, the experts, were prepared to discuss their ideas, and prepared to see their point of view. The children, certainly, have benefited, as fewer of them find teachers and parents asking them to do opposing things.

Parents in the classroom

We have not yet met with much success when we invite immigrant parents to come and help us in the classroom. They have responded well to invitations to help make library cushions, to wash dressing-up clothes, to look after school pets, or anything they can do in their homes in their own time. But most of them are at work during the day, or on night-work, and in need of rest during school hours. Even the offer of a few hours in the nursery for a toddler, while his mother helps in school, does not seem to appeal to our immigrant parents. With some mothers, especially those from Asian or Mediterranean families, the reason for not coming to school to help is quite simply that their husbands forbid it; for them a woman's place is in the home, and there she must stay. With others, the reason is because they do not see themselves as capable of acting as teachers' aides. Their attitude to teachers is one of respect, and even at times awe, and they are afraid that their own lack of knowledge might show up in school. Whenever we have persuaded a mother to come in for a little while, she seems to have enjoyed herself. Unfortunately, the added confidence that working with the teachers gives her works against us in the end, as invariably she then goes out and finds a more remunerative job for herself, and joins the ranks of working mothers.

We do have a number of non-immigrant mothers who come into school regularly to help in the classrooms, and there is a valuable lesson that they all learn. Many of our parents seem to think that children with a different coloured skin, or who speak a different language, must be different from their own children. One of the things they learn as they help us in school is that very often these despised 'immigrant kids' are among the brightest in the class. They learn that all the children in the school can be 'good', 'bad', bright or dull regardless of their origins. They talk with the London-born Nigerian child and are surprised to find that not only has he a cockney accent, but he plays the same street-games, worships the same football heroes, and watches the same TV programmes as their own child. The change of attitude in school is remarkable. I make no claims for any success in changing their attitude out of school. One mother who has helped us regularly for eighteen months now was heard in the local supermarket discussing 'all these — foreigners' with another parent. The teacher who heard her later deliberately used the same phrase in front of her in school, and was reprimanded by the parent, 'Nearly all these children were born here, they're British.' 'What about their parents then?' said the teacher, letting it be known that she had overheard the supermarket conversation, 'Oh, I didn't mean any of *our* families.' Now, can we claim a very small victory there? Is *our* better than *those?* Of course, we are aiming at a much greater change in attitudes but perhaps it is necessary to start in a small way.

An open invitation

We are always saying and writing to parents 'Come into school at any time, we are always pleased to see you.' And they come. They come just to see if we really are teaching their children, in other words to 'inspect' us, especially the better educated parents from overseas, who want to be convinced that our methods really will work with their children. Of course, our open invitation has to mean what it says, it has to mean *any* time. It means that we sometimes have to ask parents waiting half an hour too early in the hall for the end of school to stop chatting, so that their children can enjoy their music lesson, but that we must nevertheless be glad to see them there.

When the children first start school, we operate a 'staggered entry' and only admit a few children to each class each week. This means that we can ask mothers to stay for a while with their child, if necessary for several days, until the child has settled down. In this way, the teachers get to know most of the mothers quite well. I always say, when admitting a child to school, 'Please come and see me at any time if you have any problems. I am always available during school, and also until 7 p.m. every Wednesday evening.' Sometimes a parent will come directly to me with a problem, more often he or she is referred to me by the class teacher. Sometimes a parent will come into the office ostensibly to make a complaint, but really to get help over some problem. For example, Mrs L. comes in in a very aggressive mood, to complain that Kenny has lost his hat again. I send out for the hat, which is found in the lost property box, and wait to hear the real reason for the visit. Gradually Mrs L. begins to tell me her troubles. She is having difficulties with her landlord, and doesn't know where to turn for help. I ring the local citizens' advice bureau and make an appointment for her. No appointment is really necessary, but it seems to help if Mrs L. can go in and mention my name, it seems to give her confidence. I have found that very often the more aggressive the parent, the greater the problems they are facing. The lost hat, or the missing glove, is often no more than the 'key' to enter the school. After the initial occasion, such a complaint is no longer needed, and parents come in freely to ask for help and advice. It could perhaps be argued that it is no part of a headteacher's work to act as a social worker to the locality. But whatever affects the parents also affects the children. If there are difficulties at home, there are nearly always problems facing the child in school. Of course, I am not able to answer all the questions, solve all the problems. Usually, however, I can put the distraught parent in touch with the official or agency who can help. Sometimes I can write a letter or make a phone call to the appropriate office of the local authority. Whatever I do, I must first listen, and this can take a lot of time. Sometimes there is no need for any action on my part, just being able to talk to someone, having to set out the problem clearly for someone else to understand, helps the parent to see the solution for herself. Sometimes, there seems to be nothing anyone can do to help, except to offer moral support through a difficult period. Often the greatest need is for a little human sympathy and the feeling that no one is condemning or disapproving. Many of our parents have the most appalling difficulties to contend with. I have heard many stories of deserted wives and husbands, of fathers imprisoned, of yet another child on the way and no man to support the family, of arguments with other tenants of the house over who controls the water tap. There are violent husbands, absentee landlords, hire-purchase problems, sheer poverty. Somehow, for the most part the parents remain cheerful and optimistic. Perhaps my admiration for them, and the way they cope with more problems than I would care to face, shows as I talk with them; perhaps it is true that a problem shared is a problem halved; perhaps it is just the human contact they need; but it does seem that most of them leave the school feeling a little happier, a little more able to cope with their lives.

What was once the function of the village clergyman or the doctor has now, it seems, become the task of the schoolteacher. In this way the parents are asking for school to have a central function in their lives, and since we, too, are hoping that one day the school will become a community school, the least we can do is try to come up to their expectations.

Our contact with all the various social agencies operating in the neighbourhood helps us too. When we are concerned about a child's progress or behaviour in school, we usually look first for problems at home. Because they know our concern, the local health visitors or social workers often drop in to tell us about any families with problems, and we try to cooperate wherever we can. Sometimes it is better for me or one of the staff to go and visit a child's home. We are always made welcome, but inevitably the visit carries with it some sort of official overtone. If the local health visitor simply makes one of her routine calls, and incidentally mentions the child at school, while ostensibly discussing baby's progress, we can often learn a lot more.

Some conclusions

It is difficult to assess the results of our efforts in home–school relationships in concrete terms. There are a few facts and figures we can be sure of. We know at least 70 per cent of our mothers by sight, and one member of staff at least knows each mother by name. Fathers are less well known, but even I was surprised to find that we know just over 15 per cent of them by sight, and usually by name too. Considering that most fathers are at work during school hours, and that most of our immigrant fathers do not consider the details of their children's education to be their responsibility, it seems that we have made a start. All this is very cosy and friendly. It is nice to be shopping in the area at the weekends, and to be greeted by friendly faces and smiles, to be able to walk to school pleasantly gossiping with a mother and her family. However, however pleasant it all is, we also should try to assess how valuable it is in the educational process.

So far, we have found no acceptable way of testing the value of home–school contacts. The teachers *feel* that it is helpful to know as much as possible about the child's background and previous experience, that such information is helpful to them. Whether it would be just as valuable if it could be provided by someone else we don't know, but on the whole the staff feel that the continuing contact with the parents as children grow and develop is important. Whether such contacts have any effect on the children's educational process it is impossible to prove. Again, we have the *feeling* that it does, but as one teacher said when a controlled experiment was suggested, 'I am so sure of the good effects of our work with parents that I am not prepared to put any of my children at risk by not maintaining contact with their parents; not just so that you can try to prove what we already know is true.' Laudable but not scientific, perhaps, but expressing clearly what the staff think.

Certainly the staff do spend a good deal of their time and energy on contacts with parents and it could be asked whether they are justified in this, considering the amount of work that we ask of infant teachers today. Would their time be better spent in even more preparation, making apparatus, keeping abreast of new developments and the latest research in 'pure' educational activities? For us the answer is that our job would be even more difficult if we did not know our families fairly well. We are convinced that many of our children would have much greater emotional problems if their teachers and parents were not able to discuss together the best ways of dealing with a worrying situation. We have found that if a teacher is to explain an unfamiliar educational method to an immigrant parent, the teacher must be absolutely clear about its aims and ideas, must know how any drawbacks are outweighed by the advantages, and must understand completely what she is doing and why. How many teachers can honestly say that they have never taken up and applied a new method without fully understanding all its implications? Perhaps it would do us all good to have to define and if necessary defend our techniques from time to time. At the very least we find in our school that we are always revising our ideas about the educational value of some time-honoured methods and institutions.

The teachers, too, feel that they are helped by knowing the

children as individuals in an individual family. It is only too easy to begin to put the children we teach into categories, and to type them. It is well known just how damaging or helpful can be the teacher's estimation of a child's ability, and how well children tend to conform to our expectations of them. I knew one school where I was assured that all those children from the home were very difficult, and indeed, they did seem to be a problem in school. When I visited them at home, they displayed none of the signs of disturbance and truculence I had seen in school, but seemed very well adjusted and happy. Perhaps we are helped to see Alan as an individual with a particular problem, rather than as a 'difficult' child, just because we know his mother so well, and have helped her a little through a difficult time. At least Alan knows that the one stable place in his troubled existence is school, and he knows that it is to school that his mother too turns for help.

By talking to our parents we long ago found that there is no such person as a typical Cypriot, or a typical West Indian. We have widened our own horizons, and begun to see Cyprus as a collection of towns and intimate villages, to recognize the differences between the Caribbean islands, and between all the individuals from any particular island. It is difficult when trying to condense so much into so few words, not to generalize, but in our approaches to children and to their parents we have learnt not to generalize, not to prejudge attitudes, not to have our expectations all worked out beforehand.

There have often been suggestions that much of the work that teachers put into home–school relations could be better and more efficiently done by a qualified educational social worker. That may very well be so, and after a series of very exhausting interviews with parents in trouble I am certain that it is so. But at present we do not have an educational social worker, or a teacher social worker, our care committee is hopelessly overworked, and these parents cannot wait until some committee somewhere decides to provide a suitable post. In our school we are lucky in that we are sufficiently well staffed to allow us all to devote some time to work with parents, without feeling that we are neglecting other important aspects of our work. Are we justified in spending so much time on our community work? We think we are, others may think that we do not do enough, or that it would be better to use all our energies on the children, rather than including their parents. We can only answer that such is the extent to which the children are reflections of their parents that we would be wasting our time if we did not include the parents in the life of the school. We have plans to try to meet our parents sooner, long before their children start school, to try to enlist their help in talking to their children more, encouraging them to provide more play materials (cheap ones, of the junk variety) and more experiences for their children. We have already noticed how the younger brothers and sisters of children whose parents we have been able to contact are better prepared for school, better able to take advantage of the education offered to them. For the sake of the children, we cannot afford to relax our efforts.

3 Deprivation and One Infant School

Janet Eavis

Narrow streets, houses occupied by several families cheek by jowl with factories of various sorts, warehouses, pubs, shops, small family businesses, cafes, supermarkets and street market – a varied environment by any standards, picturesque maybe for those who don't have to live there but what about bringing children up in such surroundings where the greatest premium is on space? No space for trees and grass to run and stretch on, and see the open sky. Add to all this the fact that most of the property is crumbling and not safe, but a family cannot take the initiative and move away for fear of losing their place on the council re-housing list. That is the situation facing most of the families at our school. To give one typical example:

Mrs A., deserted by her husband, lives in a damp basement room with her three children and pays her landlord five pounds a week for the pleasure. The 'telly' is on the go all evening and the younger children have to try to sleep against the noise and appear bright and eager at school the next day. Mrs A. is one of those who must wait patiently until her turn comes up on the list. Meanwhile, the school must understand why her children, potentially bright, are a 'behaviour problem' because they have difficulty in adjusting to the tremendous gap between the environments of home and school.

Many other examples of the environment of a school like ours will be similar. The point to be stressed is that these conditions have been with us for many years and it would seem that authorities have been too complacent, or have just lost sight of the needs of what are conveniently called 'areas of inner urban decay'. The coming of large numbers of immigrant families into these areas has high-lighted a problem that has been there all along. In meeting the language difficulties of the immigrant children we have discovered, or perhaps begun to come to terms with, linguistic deprivation amongst the host community – children who have a 'restricted code' and who do not have an adequate model to follow from the adults in their community seem to be in a vicious circle in which they are trapped.*

The word 'deprivation' itself too often tends to become a catchall phrase which can blur and not clarify the problems of schools in educational priority areas. There are a number of specific kinds of symptoms which, in my view, all teachers in EPA schools need to learn to recognize and respond to in their teaching. One can start with the most obvious and basic point of all, symptoms of physical deprivation or neglect.

Happily, very few children who come up for routine school medical examinations nowadays are found to be under-nourished or suffering from serious physical defects. On the whole, parents do take their children of pre-school age to the infant and child welfare clinics. However, there are some children who come to school in need of medical attention of a minor nature which might indicate parental ignorance or neglect. In cases like this the school has to try to educate parents in the care of their children and get them to realize, for example, that T. (West Indian) cannot be at school with a large blister on his leg caused by steam from an electric steam iron; or B. (English) with running sores around his mouth which might be infectious and appear to have developed through neglect. Neither can children return to school too soon after some of the usual infectious diseases of childhood. It is interesting to note that the ignorance and neglect mentioned is common to children of both English and immigrant parents in our school, which is an 'educational priority area'. Parents from both groups often *have* to go to work and accommodation is so overcrowded that one is led to think that they feel that their children will be better off at school. The experience of a qualified nursery assistant or helper with some elementary knowledge of first aid is invaluable to the staffs of schools where these problems are a daily occurrence. There is need for the training and appointment of such people. One authority (ILEA) ran a short course one morning a week for a period in a college of further education which was immensely popular with its participants, who were infant helpers.

* For further examination of this subject, see Denis Lawton, *Social Class, Language and Education*, Routledge & Kegan Paul, 1968.

We often have good reason to believe that some children come to school with little or no breakfast. It is not unusual to see children from certain families buying buns and sweets before school in the morning. When the milk is delivered to the classroom about half an hour after school has begun, some children cannot wait until 'playtime' for it. Even when one has allowed for the normal appetites of growing children there is strong evidence to show that feeding at home is somewhat erratic. It would appear that the reasons are not always economic since some of these children, we know, are from families where money is not short. But because both parents are working full-time and on shifts that do not fit easily with children's needs, time to deal with the children is limited. Under these circumstances, it is easier to give the children money to buy fish and chips than make meals which constitute a balanced diet. Parents do not always realize how important feeding is in relation to general health, and many mothers have to use most inadequate kitchen facilities. We try to improve these conditions for the children through the school, e.g. by the school doctor, at the routine medical inspections, informal meetings for mothers, visits from health visitors and health education officers, and through posters and leaflets. But as always, it is difficult to make contact with those parents who never come to school because they are working. Perhaps we should be more positive about parental involvement and make it harder for them to opt out.*

Poor health and hunger are relatively easy to detect. But recognizing the other problems that children have, on entry to school and afterwards, calls for great understanding and skill on the part of the head and the class teacher. It is safe to assume that those children who show persistent behaviour of aggression, withdrawal or constantly seek attention will have some good reason for doing so. An investigation into the background at home or at the previous school will sometimes bring results and throw light on the underlying circumstances that are the root of the difficulty. Because of this, when children are admitted to

* See, for example, J. and E. Newson, *Patterns of Infant Care in an Urban Community*, Penguin, 1965, and the follow-up, *Four Years Old in an Urban Community*, Penguin, 1970.

school, we attempt to gain as much information as possible about the child's personal history and the family background. Parents are usually very willing to relate their histories. Often this can take a long time but we feel it is time well spent. We ask, for instance, if the child has ever been away from home for any prolonged times. The following case will show why it is important to ask this question.

T. was admitted to school at a rising five. Her parents, from Jamaica, were separated but her father was maintaining her. The mother was very shy about her marital state and casually mentioned at the interview that T. had been in a foster home in the country since she was nine months old. When she was old enough to come to school her father wanted her to come back to her mother, perhaps for financial reasons. It was not long before her teacher was reporting that T. was behaving in a rather strange way. She was aggressive, began to 'steal' things in the classroom, was withdrawn and showing every sign of being extremely insecure. We felt that this could very well be a result of the child's pre-school history. She was almost certainly attached to her foster parents from whom she had been uprooted to live with comparative strangers and on top of this she had to come to school and to adjust to another new situation. It was, therefore, not at all surprising that T. behaved as she did. Because she had been in a secure situation at school with a sympathetic teacher, who knew her background, this child has made great progress. She has begun to read at five and a half and her social behaviour is normal for her age.

Information built up over a period of time and passed on to the next school is essential reference material particularly when there is any serious problem and we take great pains to do this whenever our children move. I can illustrate this with an example of one of the difficulties which occur when there are no records. Mobility is the most common characteristic of deprived children, and often they are not in one place for long enough for a school to acquire any adequate records.

A. came to the nursery class and a few weeks after admission had what was described as a 'funny turn' in the playground. The mother was asked if there had ever been any previous history of epilepsy or convulsions. She had not noticed anything of the kind before except violent temper tantrums. Because the family had moved so many times and in different parts of the country, the medical records for this child could not be traced. It is still not certain whether this child has a history of convulsions and the matter has not been closed as there is a known sibling history.

There are, however, inherent dangers in using the information gained from interviews with parents and other sources such as health visitors and records from previous schools. It is very easy to be prejudiced into seeing nothing but the problems and getting them out of perspective. The essential thing is to keep the *whole* child in mind.

B. came to school at four plus from extremely overcrowded home conditions: mother and father from Jamaica, trying their best to do well for the family of five of which B. was the fourth. Both parents worked and the children were often left in charge of the older brother, himself at an E S N school. When B. came to school he was brought by the brother and neither parent was seen. B. showed no sign at all of communicating with anyone and for several weeks did nothing but play with sand and water which he was able to do happily in a class-room that was run on the principle of a 'free day'. But it was obvious that this child was urgently in need of help which the school was not qualified to give. The services of the educational psychologist were brought in and as a result this child has had psychotherapy and teaching in a tutorial class for a year. He is now beginning to read and talks reasonably well to adults and children. He has found a great outlet in painting and other creative work which he performs at a standard well above average for his age.

In the case of B. one of the most happy outcomes has been the relationship that has grown up between the parents and the school. At first they were afraid to come at all, but because they were taken by the health visitor to the child guidance clinic, they gradually gained confidence to come into school. B.'s younger brother entered the nursery class which meant the mother had to come to school daily. It is a slow and delicate process to build up relationships but we feel it is worth all the time and patience necessary over and over again.

A Greek Cypriot boy came to school, the second child of a family of three, the eldest being a boy and the youngest a girl. The father made a great fuss of the eldest boy and whole family made much of the girl, so this child was left out. He was most aggressive in class and in the playground, fighting and kicking and destroying work done by other children. He talked very little and in any case English is a second language for him – quite enough strain, without the added emotional problems. We have very flexible age grouping so it was possible to let this child stay with the same teacher for two years. She built up an excellent relationship with him, slowly gaining his confidence to the point when he felt assured that he did not have to kick and scream to get her attention. He began to learn to read before transferring to the junior school and there the same approach has been continued and he can read fluently at nine. His sister, who has been in the school since she was four, now at seven plus has a reading age of nine.

The personality of the teacher and her ability to create a warm, caring atmosphere around her is vital. Many teachers, especially of young children, have this ability, in fact, they are often mothers of young children themselves. The basis of all that happens in the classroom and the success and progress of the children depend so much on the relationship between teacher and child.

One of the most generally recognized problems in EPA infant schools is the lack of normal play experience of many children, caused equally by the neighbourhood, overcrowded housing and the lack of leisure of parents. It is a continuing shock to teachers when they discover just how limited is the experience of everyday life and objects to children in deprived areas. A student teacher, working with us, arranged to take her class on the underground and discovered that, even though most of the children lived only a few minutes walk from the tube station, hardly any of them had ever been there. We have also taken children to parks not too far from their homes to show them for the first time, common-place birds, animals and flowers, such as ducks and squirrels. In school it is comparatively easy to compensate for the lack of experience outside the immediate environment by frequently arranging visits to be followed up in the classroom with creative work and discussion, all of which will mean extension of the children's language. Stimulation comes from this kind of shared experience and gives both teacher and children a common ground. These visits need not be elaborate and costly. There is much to be seen in the immediate locality of the school to which frequent and short visits can be made. For instance, a disused piece of land behind an old church near the school became a happy hunting ground for all kinds of treasures, such as insects, worms and flowers. The looks on the faces of children who on that occasion picked flowers for the first time was worth seeing. Visits to local shopkeepers are another way of helping children to look at their environment and to appreciate it and talk about it. Some infant children including several immigrants, Greek and West Indian, were taken shopping in the lunch hour and went to the butcher. They had no idea what meat looked like all of a piece, hung up in whole carcasses, and this experience brought many questions and discussion. We have been convinced of the necessity to be aware of ways and means of stimulating the children into developing their senses to the full. All the senses are involved but perhaps only the obvious ones of sight and sound are given adequate attention and such things as the tactile are neglected. To feel things, to touch and to talk about the feel of pebbles, or velvet or the fur of an animal are experiences all children need to have. Collections of things in school help here – groups of objects which have something in common, e.g. the same colour, made of similar material such as mats, baskets, hats made from straw. The children enjoy helping to collect these things and arranging them.

In all our classrooms the following basic materials are provided to give children the experiences many of them have never had at home: sand (wet and dry); clay; wood and tools; paint, mixed thickly, and large paper to give satisfactory results and sense of real achievement; plenty of junk of all kinds, i.e. cartons, magazines, egg boxes, apple boxes from the greengrocer made from polystyrene; wire netting for making models; plenty of materials left from dressmaking (some nearby dress factories oblige); suitable glues that will really stick; newspaper, old wallpaper samples and left over rolls; cotton reels; odd pieces of plastic and cardboard, and boxes of varying sizes and shapes.

Poor accommodation, overcrowding and ignorance of the needs of young children, we feel, are responsible for the deprivation which is all too evident in most of our five year olds on entry to school. Some cases are more extreme than others and easier to recognize. But when teachers are aware of the problems, and sensitive about meeting children's developing needs, the children can develop in a remarkable way.

C. is a Jamaican boy of almost six years who came to the nursery class at four. He is the youngest of a family of five in this country and there are more at home in Jamaica. His parents are separated and his mother appears to do casual jobs such as baby-minding and cleaning. They live in a slum property which is occupied by other families as well as C.'s family.

When C. was brought to the nursery class at four by his mother, he was morose, slow physically, had a dull glazed look in his eyes, had little or nothing to say but was obedient and obviously expected that his role as a child was to be quiet and still. Two years later, in the infant class, after plenty of experience with creating and painting, with listening and talking, with learning to read and write his own stories, he is bright of eye, alert and quick and responsive. He is musical and responds well to music, rhythm and singing. In every respect, he has progressed out of dullness and apathy to the point where he is aware of the world around and his curiosity is for ever taking him into new experiences and learning. Once a child has been aroused in this way, there is no holding him and one is hopeful that he may go on to realize his full potential at a later age.

We know from the work of Piaget that children must pass through the stages of development in sequence. In our school, very often we find children who, on entry to school, are still at the pre-sensori-motor stage. Therefore, the classroom must provide for the child's development at this stage and the material must be structured to this end. We have decided this is best done by dividing the room into areas which cater for various parts of learning and play. Some classrooms were easier to transform than others but we have at least improved them and made more relevant to the needs of our children by dividing them one way or another. Much is being done by our authorities to improve old buildings along these lines. We try to work to the following plan which can be adapted to meet individual needs and resources.

A home area with wendy house, dressing-up box, etc.	A language arts area for reading and writing
Creative area with paints, clay, etc.	A mathematical area

We have found that when the arrangement described is set up it makes it easier for the programme of the day to be more flexible because things are to hand and do not have to be got out of cupboards at special times. Children share in the responsibility for the care and tidiness of the classroom and they learn this quite quickly once they see the sound sense behind it. The teacher plans for the varying needs and interests of the children. However, the free and flexible arrangement which allows us to pay maximum attention to each child's individual needs carries problems for a small number of children: let me take one example.

D. is a live wire. He came to the nursery at four years and two years later is still full of unresolved aggression. He is the second child and only boy in a family of five. He is quite wild and uncontrolled when an unfamiliar situation blows up, for example, if his teacher is absent. He seeks attention constantly, we think because he gets little at home. He is terribly enthusiastic about playing games either in the playground or classroom, e.g. snap, snakes and ladders, but these games usually end in disaster for his friends because of his insistence on winning by all possible means. D. is difficult to handle in a classroom which is structured to give the children as much outlet for their frustrations and needs as possible. When he is in these wild moods the only solution that has been found to be successful is to isolate him from other children and for a sympathetic adult to keep him usefully occupied until he has literally calmed down.

We know that children like D. are to be found in all schools. The rural or suburban schools often can point to similar children. Children like this are not restricted to one social class. But when this kind of behaviour is added to poor home conditions, either physical or emotional, or both, plus language difficulties, teachers are hard-pressed to know what to do with children who sometimes appear to be near disintegration. When they first enter school in the infant school or nursery class it has been found that, for children who come from homes where there is little or no opportunity for creative and imaginative play, the rich environment of a classroom set out in this stimulating way, giving freedom of space and choice of activity, is quite overwhelming and does have disastrous effects upon some children. Some of our children withdraw and just gaze while others go quite berserk. To stagger our intake we admit a few children only at a time, twice a week at the beginning of a new term until the intake is absorbed in both nursery and infant classes. This gives the teacher the chance to get to know a few new children at a time and for them to get used to the classroom. Not all the equipment is introduced to new children all at once. We no longer have a reception class. This means that new children enter a class that already exists with children who are familiar with school. We have come to believe that a reception class in the September term with all new five year olds and possibly a new teacher is asking too much of the resources of both teacher and children. By avoiding this situation, there is less risk of having to cope with unhappy, berserk children. We have found that the West Indian and Nigerian children have reacted particularly strongly to this rich environment and free atmosphere at school. They seem to come from homes, in England, where discipline is different, perhaps stricter, and the contrast between this and the free atmosphere of our infant school is more than many of them can take. This does not mean that the approach we were accustomed to use in the classroom is thrown out, but it means that it has to be more carefully organized and introduced more gradually. Chaos is not allowed to reign and children know this and seem to feel secure within this framework.

One field in which infant teachers obviously have a particular claim to interest is in developing the basic linguistic skills. In any school with immigrant pupils this work will have an extra dimension. Some still argue that immigrant children to whom English is a second language will just pick up the language in the classroom. Experience and various tests (e.g. the National Literacy Survey) just do not bear this out in practice and many teachers have now realized this. Language teaching for all children must be central to all that takes place in the infant school, but we have realized that the teacher has consciously to put the language into the situation. Some children get by fairly well, enough to make teachers think that, although English is not their first or home language, they can read it and use it. Then one day, words taken out of context, words needed to describe actions and things around which are not so familiar, throw these children into difficulty. It is then that we realize that more needs to be done than just hoping that language is 'picked up'.

K., aged five and a half, Greek Cypriot, came to school at four and a half with very little command of English although she has cousins who are older in the school who speak well, and her parents who have lived in Britain for some years are reasonably fluent in English. K. was reading to me from the Ladybird 3a book in which there are pictures of children playing about in boats. This prompted her to burst forth into a long talk about a family excursion to a local park with a boating lake. She said, 'We went in a boat like that and me auntie had one of those (great hesitation here and pointing at the oar in the picture) and she nearly dropped it in the water and we went to the end and we crashed in the . . . (again hesitation) . . .' and so the tale went on helped with the naming of places and objects for which she did not have sufficient vocabulary.

The situation I have described is a frequent experience, not only for our children to whom English is a second language, but also for many of our mother-tongue children. I use this anecdote to illustrate how, in our experience, it is essential to provide the maximum opportunities for the children to form a close relationship with adults with whom they can talk. The teacher provides an encouraging ear and this situation of talk is used to extend their vocabulary and oral skills in English. The situation is a replica of the situation frequently occurring between mother and child at home. We try to organize our classes and the whole school so that our children can talk and be talked with as much as possible.

The difficulty for many teachers with large classes with a high proportion of children needing specific help with language is to be able to give sufficient individual teaching and attention. We have used part-time teachers, students and others to help relieve the situation in the classroom by taking out small groups either for specific teaching or to relieve the class teacher so that she can help those in most need. Basic skills are taught in these small groups, i.e. phonic work, word games and practice in the structures of English. When this has been done regularly and systematically the children have made progress. The value of small groups enabling children to form a close and more intimate relationship with an adult cannot be overestimated. In smaller groups it is possible to develop children's powers of concentration, the skill of listening and the chance to talk and be listened to by the adult.

All the problems I have briefly described here are caused basically by situations outside the school and the education service, and are practically beyond the power of teachers to prevent or control. Yet within a deprived area, schools have the power to make a contribution to the wider community over and above their statutory duties. In one way at least, we have found that the extra effort involved in doing this has brought its own rewards when we are back in the classroom in our more strictly professional role: this has been our play centre.

Play centres attached to primary schools have been established for many years within the London Education Service. They came into being during the war when it was necessary for children to be in a known safe place whilst their parents were working long hours in a national emergency. They remained as part of the service after the war and are open during term and holiday times. They are staffed by people who have various interests and skills to offer to children and amongst them are many teachers. In some schools, where either the head or another teacher has been involved in the running of the play centre over a period of time it is natural for the organization to flow over into the normal school activities, and in some cases to become an extension of them for the two or so hours after school when the play centre takes place. The Plowden Report, in its recommendations at the end of chapter 4 on the educational priority areas, says that community schools should be tried out first in priority areas. The ILEA has done this in respect of some twenty or so schools where play centres were already in existence. This is how we came to be running our school community centre. We began by taking over the play centre which was already housed in our school.

The centre was attended at the time when we took it over by some twenty to thirty children from the whole of the primary-school age group, i.e. from five to eleven years, and was available from the end of school until 6 p.m. The infants were catered for in one group and the juniors grouped according to interest and availability of staff. There were no teachers on the staff of the play centre.

We felt that the success of the venture depended on the willingness of teachers to cooperate and those who could be spared from other commitments readily agreed to help. This means that in order to cover the play centre times of opening, teachers work for two evenings in the centre for which they are paid under the rates laid down by the authority. The centre is open every evening during term-time except Fridays. At first, the teachers found the strain of working for two hours after normal school was quite considerable. The centre aims to provide a safe place for children to play under supervision with adequate, suitable equipment and materials. It is not quite the same as a classroom situation no matter how flexible and informal that may be. The change for the infant children is not as great as for the older juniors. Our teachers soon became accustomed to a different way of working and the advantages of work with the play centre have proved to be enormous.

The basic materials that are provided by the local authority include sand, clay, paint, water, writing and drawing materials, books; games such as ludo, snakes and ladders, chess, etc.; large toys, i.e. tricycles, scooters, construction toys; dressing-up and wendy house with dolls, etc.; large bricks, slide, table tennis and shuttlecock and football. There are also opportunities for needlework and crafts on the evenings when teachers of these particular interests are present. Children can learn to dance and television is also available. The children who want to stay forgather each afternoon when school closes with the staff who are on duty that evening and we have a snack tea. After this they are free to play – either indoors or sometimes outside in the playground if the weather is fine. There are usually three groups of activities going on each evening, one with infants, possibly junior boys playing football and another group of juniors playing indoor games, watching television or doing craft work, etc. Fortunately, the school is in a recently re-modelled building, with a large hall which is used almost exclusively for dinners in the day-time, and for the play centre in the evening. There are places where children can withdraw when they want to have quieter activities. The school has joined with other play centres in the area in a play centre football league which is never short of supporters. Children who transfer to secondary schools sometimes come in to visit their old friends.

The advantages of running a community centre along these lines are considerable in an area of special need where all the difficulties of children and their families mentioned previously are overwhelming. We have found that the relationships between teachers and children, junior and infant school, parents and teachers, have grown closer, as a result there is more confidence and security for many children. The shared staffing and facilities between the infant and junior schools has made the experience of transfer at seven much easier. Because there are not two sets of staff (good as these may be) working with children, their loyalties are not divided and they feel more secure. Parents who we would rarely see otherwise come to school to meet their children after working hours at the play centre. Children of parents who are not working stay because the parents and children appreciate the opportunity to make use of the facilities provided which are not available within the immediate area of most homes. There are no parks nearby without crossing busy roads. Street football has its attractions but is a poor alternative to the space of the school playground.

When we started hardly any immigrant children stayed for the play centre. Some just did not know about it, others thought it was only for working mothers (an attitude which has taken a long time to break down with all parents) and others never thought about it. There is no doubt that for those to whom English is a second language, particularly the Cypriot children, the extension of the school day and the opportunity to be within an English-speaking environment for this extra time, has made a significant difference to their competence in English. It must be pointed out that at no time, has pressure been put on parents or children to attend. Some children attend for only an hour and some come once or twice a week whilst others stay the whole time every day. None the less, it is important to ensure that all parents are aware of facilities of this kind, where they and their children will be welcomed in a convenient place, and a friendly and familiar atmosphere.

I have tried to give a brief and simple account of some attempts that we have made to overcome the difficulties that teachers face in meeting the varying needs of children in the schools in the educational priority areas. Underlying all the suggestions I would particularly stress the importance of the whole school community and the relationships within it. Experience has shown us that when parents and children feel that they are included in all that goes on, when they see that there are goals that can be achieved; when they can begin to feel that it is not a question of 'them and us' then there is the beginning of a break through the traditional attitude that so many working-class parents have towards school. This is not an easy matter and it cannot be structured by the laying down of a simple formula applicable to all situations. Each school community has to find its own way and to make the most of each opportunity when it arises.

4 The Changing Response of a Secondary Modern School in Handsworth, 1958–1970

George Meredith

During the first two or three years when our school became a multi-racial one, the predominant feeling of the teachers was one of considerable dismay. Pupils from Jamaica and India began to arrive in large numbers in the summer term of 1959, a year after the school had changed from a well-established boys' secondary modern school to a co-educational one. By 1961 about a third of the pupils were from overseas. From 1963 the numbers of these children increased steadily until by 1966 they formed some 60 per cent of the school population, and by 1969 about 65 per cent. At this point about 45 per cent of our 550 pupils were of West Indian origin, about 20 per cent were Sikhs from the Punjab and Africa, and the remainder English.

The memory of those first years is still vivid and I can recall clearly the concern and dismay at the turn events had taken. The establishment of a new school in old buildings, with two other schools housed in bright new buildings a mile away, was in any case a struggle. The fact that we had accommodation to spare for the new pupils presenting themselves daily seemed a doubtful blessing. But the interest and enthusiasm of the devoted staff was encouraging and we were all optimistic for the future.

A period of breakdown

The development of the school went through a number of stages. The first two or three years, until 1962, I would describe as a period of breakdown.

This seems to be an appropriate title since much of what we had learnt, experienced and enjoyed disappeared. We were thrust without warning into a situation for which we knew no solutions, indeed we only knew the problems as they steadily grew more severe. New attitudes, organizations and techniques had to be evolved. Yet the business of the school had to continue, ensuring that the children whose needs we understood did not suffer.

Good, experienced teachers found that their skills were suddenly inadequate for this new situation; often they found themselves having to teach groups whose educational background was inadequate, or having to deal with behaviour problems of a completely new kind. The loss of prestige suffered by the school was felt keenly and the difficulty of adjusting to a completely new school community with different qualities was a great strain. Many school social and recreational activities foundered through lack of support. Often parents would not allow children to participate in activities outside normal school time. The first problem was therefore one of morale, since any loss of morale was bound to be reflected in our attitudes to the children and the school. After many discussions it was clear that we had first to declare *to ourselves* that we accepted the new situation: that any member of staff who could not accept it, and the challenge involved, was perfectly free to accept or refuse the appointment. Thirdly it had to be accepted that the school was a multi-racial one in a multi-racial community: that we had to establish a new concept of the place and function of such a school, for the benefit of the children who were the victims of this situation.

During this first period two main problems quickly emerged.

1. The difficulties posed by numbers of non-English-speaking children.

2. The presence of considerable numbers of Jamaican children who lacked the educational background normally expected from our pupils, on which our standards, curriculum and teaching methods were based.

Some help was available with the first group by the provision of a small force of peripatetic language teachers who visited schools for two or three half-days a week. As the numbers of immigrant children grew, the situation became much more serious, with not only an intensification of the actual problems but resentment and hostility from the local population, and anxiety among the English parents about the education of their own children. There were very strong queries about the ability of schools to cope both with the needs of the immigrant pupils and those of the local children, and it was always our great concern to ensure that the needs of each did not conflict.

The difficulties of organization were enormous, yet it was vital to find a structure to work efficiently. The school was organized at this time on a streamed basis and the weight of numbers in the lower streams became a source of great concern. Indeed, it became difficult to maintain any structure as admissions were continuous. It was not unusual to find a bulge developing in a particular age group during the course of the year with consequent teaching difficulties. The two main groups – Indian and West Indian – seemed to us to pose completely different problems.* The question of the teaching day and specialist instruction was also a problem since, although it was impossible for many to follow a full range of subjects, they could not be kept on basic work all day. The needs of the local children also had to be kept in the forefront. Two main problems seemed incompatible: socially it seemed undesirable to maintain streaming since the lower streams were predominately coloured and the upper streams were predominately white; on the other hand, clearly the needs of many immigrant children required special teaching and organization.

It was decided at this stage to abandon streaming, but to retain facilities for 'setting' in English, maths and science, together with a special remedial department of two units – one for non-English-speaking children and one for severely backward West Indians, each containing about forty children. As children progressed they were filtered from this department into classes. It also served as a reception for new arrivals. Although segregation was a word often used at this time with unpleasant connotations, it was felt that this arrangement would best serve the varying needs of the pupils. During the next three years the remedial department was a substantial one and for some time it was felt that specialist subjects could not be usefully taught to these pupils until they had reached certain basic standards. The head of this department was one of the senior posts in the school.

* Since then there has been more work done on the specific language difficulties of Caribbean immigrant pupils. See 'Teaching English to West Indian Children: The Research Stage of the Project', Evans-Methuen Educational, Schools Council Publication, 1970. See also Chapter 1.

Curricula

As more children from overseas came into the school it became clear that our educational thinking would need revision; our teaching method and the syllabus content were geared to the educational background of English children, which the immigrant children lacked. This raised particular difficulties in subjects like mathematics, science and craftwork, especially when trying to place pupils of thirteen and fourteen into suitable classes when they lacked essential groundwork. Also much of our social-science syllabus, written for English children, seemed inappropriate for multi-racial classes. The teaching of English posed problems with Jamaican children as well as Sikh children, as their vocabulary, phraseology and accent often caused difficulties through misunderstanding by pupils and teachers.

Changes were made to try to find some workable solutions. For example, science lessons based on hygiene, health education and biology were introduced for classes containing larger proportions of immigrant pupils. It seemed easier to find a common starting point in these subjects for pupils without the usual background of science teaching; also many of the girls were very keen to become nurses, so it appeared to be more appropriate to their motivation. Various changes were made in the social sciences, which included studies of the homelands of the immigrant pupils by all the children in the classes, and all children accepted these changes quite happily.

However, we had to remember that when the pupils were ready to leave school they would have to compete for jobs with English children and would need the same educational qualifications for apprenticeships and the other most sought after occupations. With such a very large proportion of children whose educational standards were below those normally expected, it was clear that somehow we had to raise the basic levels in all subjects. It was not easy to recognize potential, still more difficult to provide the right stimulus to develop it.

The school community

The task of welding three differing groups of children into a single community with a sense of belonging seemed at times impossible: the composition of the groups was constantly changing and with each group of arrivals the same ground had to be covered: the pattern of school life had to be learned over and over again by children and parents. Many times we witnessed the painful experience of parents getting to know their children after long periods of separation, and showing frustration and bitter disappointment at their children's lack of success or difficult behaviour.

In school, most of our troubles seemed at first to concern the West Indian girls. The boys seemed to be able to get release from their frustrations in physical activity and excitement. But the girls seemed sullen, insolent and quarrelsome. The response of both boys and girls to our traditional relationship between teachers and pupils was to abuse or deride it. We tried talking to individual parents – almost always to be given the advice 'beat her, teacher'. We also tried arranging separate meetings with West Indian and Indian parents. Attendance was practically nil, and we discovered that none of the parents thought they had special difficulties, different from groups of local children.

The trouble was that most of the teachers were not trained to handle the situation, in which the first essential was to keep cool, and remember that 'abnormal' behaviour was *normal*. It was not easy to identify the different reasons for rebellious behaviour, and yet retain sympathy for the pupils. It was annoying that when school activities were mounted which involved all groups, immigrant parents often refused to allow their children to participate, and sometimes children seemed to show an irritating lack of loyalty to a team or group by failing to turn up.

Most of us were aware, through experience in other schools without coloured pupils, that difficulties might be experienced through lack of interest, hostility to authority, adults and education or through lack of interest by the parents. We consoled ourselves during this period with the knowledge that our problems were not *worse* than, although they were *different* from, those we might have experienced elsewhere.

In spite of setbacks, efforts to promote a corporate spirit proceeded bravely. Progress sometimes happened by accident. One day a group of West Indian girls were discovered singing some of their folk songs in a cloakroom. From this, a West Indian Girls'

Choir was formed. And from then on, children of different races began to demonstrate their skills to each other in dance, physical education, story telling and drama, and with each tiny step greater confidence was gained by teachers as well as pupils.

One interesting social experience is worth recording. A fifth-year group of some thirty pupils of English, Jamaican and Indian origin participated in a week's 'Life and Leisure' residential course sponsored by a local voluntary organization. The course was held at a Youth Leaders' Training Centre some ten miles from the city and was run by the Association of Boys' Clubs Training Officers, and members of the school staff. The gain in mutual respect and understanding, of regard and affection for each other characterized this group for the remainder of their school life.

Another influence on the school community at this time was the effect of parental hopes on the pupils, particularly in vocational aspirations. Girls wished to become nurses or secretaries; boys saw themselves as electrical or mechanical engineers. Such ambitions were difficult enough to fulfil, and impossible for the majority of these pupils: to parents and children this frustration and disappointment left its mark with apathy and resentment. Parents, I believe, felt that school failed them: pupils felt let-down by school and parents. It was no consolation to tell them that non-academic whites could not all qualify for such jobs, but could get other well-paid jobs in industry: nor could they understand the age limitations on entry into apprenticeships. The result was that many boys and girls felt they were the victims of discrimination when they failed to secure the kind of job they wanted. This knowledge increased our desire to achieve higher basic standards with younger children, to enable as many as possible to reach the required level. I feel sure that many of those older earlier immigrants, who are now young adults, still feel embittered and frustrated.

In retrospect I am sure that although we had the best of intentions, and a genuine desire to help, we failed to understand the position of the parents, just as we failed to understand the needs of their children. As we got to grips and the organizational problems were eased, we felt that the other most urgent need was to create a happy environment where the children would feel

secure. It was repeatedly stressed that in the school community
we all had equal rights: that we would not tolerate prejudice, that
children must learn to live, work and play together, and that the
school would treat all children alike, regardless of colour. This
was of course an 'assimilation' policy, although we did not realize
it at the time. We in return expected conformity of behaviour,
and responses to the teachers' endeavours for the children. We
were of course disappointed.

A period of progress

Greater confidence developed over the next few years as numerous issues became clearer. The harrowing experience of seeing
familiar patterns crumble, without being able to see anything
beyond, became less painful. With more specialist help and a
greater understanding of the pupils, the difficulties surrounding
the non-English-speaking Sikh pupils began to reveal a brighter
side. It was soon quite obvious that many of them were highly
intelligent, and that in the main they were very industrious and
responsible.

One very interesting activity was undertaken with the assistance of a remedial specialist on the staff of the Educational
Psychologists Department. This was a simple unscientific, rough
and ready survey of all the Sikh children for whom English was a
second language, to see if we could make some estimation of their
potential. There was no intention of making any absolute comparisons with other groups: indeed, we were quite open minded
about what – if anything – might be revealed. The most we hoped
for was to be able to predict the possible capabilities of pupils in
the group relative to each other. A variety of tests were used to
build up a picture: sometimes an interpreter had to be used when
dealing with children whose English was very limited.

The results were most interesting. They suggested that there
was a higher proportion of intelligent children than would be
normal among English children in a non-selective school: they
also confirmed what we already felt – that many of them would
have passed into selective schools in normal circumstances. As a
result of this survey a number of children were placed immediately in higher groups *regardless of their level of English*. This
encouraged them enormously and stimulated their desire to

attain satisfactory standards in English. Subsequent results justified this action and teachers' attitudes took a further significant move forward. They became more disposed to look for signs of potential and less conscious of the problems. Taking CSE results as a guide, the ultimate success of many of these pupils was very pleasing and gratifying. One boy obtained five Grade One passes in CSE, including English, and many went on to further education with considerable distinction.

These results made one point clear: we had to look for potential, capitalize on the intelligence, industry and perseverance and cooperative temperament of the pupil. Good teaching methods, adaptation of schemes of work to meet particular situations and the response of the pupils seemed to offer together a solution to some of our problems.

The numbers of Indian and West Indian children throughout this period remained roughly equally balanced. These successes with the Indian children – roughly half our coloured pupils – encouraged us to feel that similar progress might be achieved with the West Indian pupils. Efforts at improving standards in basic education were redoubled. It was realized that this meant starting at early primary level with many children and for a long time it was necessary to provide what was virtually a primary-school department within the school. However, progress on this front was maintained, as well as in efforts to create a happy and well-adjusted school community. Whilst there was still resentment against the immigrant pupils from the local English population, it was interesting to see that as parents realized that the education of their own children was not suffering as they had feared and that the children appeared to get on well together, tensions seemed to ease.

Other encouraging and interesting factors were revealed during this period, one in particular concerning staffing. Publicity was a constantly recurring factor and in some ways this proved helpful, since many teachers came to the city specifically to help in this teaching emergency. The school obtained the services of many dedicated teachers during this period who deliberately chose to join the staff. I recall a teacher who had been in Israel teaching English: when she returned to the city she asked specifically to be appointed to a school with immigrant pupils. We also enjoyed the services of numerous other devoted teachers, including some from Canada and the United States who elected to work in the school because of their desire to help in this difficult situation. It was very encouraging to find teachers asking to share in our work.

Gradually enthusiasm, confidence and morale began to rise with each successive step forward, however small, and with each minor achievement. The principle of complete involvement of all departments was fully accepted and the search for new and more appropriate methods of presentation of the work in all subjects continued and was regarded as a challenge. Everyone recognized the importance of reducing the need for separate special groups, but rather to move children into 'normal' teaching situations as quickly as possible. The presence of large numbers in special teaching groups perhaps indicated that we had not fully appreciated the need for quite fundamental changes in the policy of the school. Rather, I imagine, we hoped that the remedial department would condition the children to respond to what we regarded as a normal situation: in other words we still expected the children to make all the adjustments. Gradually the remedial department was phased down. Throughout the whole period every change or development had been preceded by anxious discussion and analysis. It is interesting to look back on these earlier days and recall the moves and changes, often made without our fully understanding the significance of what we were doing in relation to the wider issues.

Nevertheless this was considered a period of progress and we felt that educational standards were rising. Substantial progress was made in literacy through programmes of concentrated efforts in first- and second-year classes, and in science the adjustments made in syllabus and method seemed to produce a better response. The general feeling was one of greater optimism, and morale rose. The school was certainly not an unhappy teaching environment: there was good humour, often excitement, and no lack of interest by the world outside in the fortunes and activities of the school. However great the staff turnover, determination, cooperation and mutual help still united us in our determination to succeed.

New problems, 1967 to the present

In earlier years we had sustained ourselves by thinking – in hindsight naïvely – that things would get better. We thought that as the rate of immigration declined, and more children came into the secondary school with the benefit of a primary education in this country the coloured children would achieve better educational standards, would be better adjusted to their environment, and would present fewer problems at secondary level. Encouraged by increasing knowledge and experience, and by moving into a new building in 1966, hopes were high. We were still able to recruit staff, and fill key posts with first-class people. Two other factors influenced us at this time.

1. The building was not completed until 1967, so that accommodation was limited and we admitted very few immigrant pupils from 1966–7. This gave us a period of stability.

2. The Birmingham Education Committee established reception centres for non-English-speaking pupils of secondary age so that none of these pupils were admitted directly into the school.

Some progress had been made in raising general standards and the principles of involvement of all departments with the lower ability groups was fully accepted. Certain practical difficulties of organization still remained however which resulted in another change in structure. The main problems were as follows:

1. Maintaining a 'setting' structure was difficult when staff shortages occurred in particular subjects by teachers leaving during the educational year.

2. In order to give them maximum opportunities, many immigrant pupils had to change 'set' or 'group' too frequently for our liking.

3. It was important that for a pupil to have a chance of achieving CSE in certain subjects, especially the technical subjects like science and mathematics, he should be transferred to an appropriate group during or by the third year.

4. We were not really happy with the mixed-ability class structure: it was difficult to maintain a balance between boys and

girls, and between abilities: the creation of a group atmosphere was not helped by the great range in ability and maturity.

A close scrutiny of all children's progress was undertaken, and serious efforts were made to estimate potential. The conclusion was reached that some 35–40 per cent only would be capable of following a course leading to CSE and that the remainder could best be helped by a broad general education, with 'Newsom'-type courses for the older pupils. This led to a two-band structure – an upper and a lower ability band. As we were now a four-form entry school each band contained two random grouped classes. The lower level of the top ability band was set low enough to contain all with the remotest possibility of achieving CSE standards. Timetable facilities for setting in English, maths and science within the two upper-band classes were retained.

During the year 1966–7 this arrangement went ahead and indications were that it was a satisfactory arrangement. Reappraisal of curricula was a repeating activity, and availability of better facilities led us again to re-examine this in the light of our greater experience. The great problem still remaining was that of the older children from overseas who could not follow a full CSE course. Examinations were still the overriding motivating force at this time. It would be no exaggeration to say that it seemed that pupils were more concerned about being allowed to sit the examination than they were about the result. During 1966–7 we had a group of some thirty immigrant 'over-age' pupils not able to follow a full CSE course. A good broad general programme was arranged for them with opportunities to sit a limited number of subjects in CSE chosen from a new 'English for immigrants' CSE examination, human biology, art, religious knowledge, home economics, crafts. A great deal of valuable and scarce teaching resources were deployed in small-group teaching to try to attain success with them. The result was disappointing: for two terms teachers met apathy, indolence and indifference, hardly a spark of real motivation was fired, and the group seemed content to amble gently along without any real effort. Following this experience one wondered whether pupils below a certain level of attainment should be allowed to continue after statutory leaving age. It was difficult however to deny pupils arriving at the age of fourteen or fifteen opportunities of at least a general education. Although fewer in number, such pupils were allowed to follow a one year's general education course. The lack of effort and response from a group of older pupils was however more significant than we at first realized.

Fourth-year non-examination pupils now came in for our special attention. Using vocational interests as the motivating force, broader based courses were arranged. The courses included one day a week at an education committee craft centre for either 'engine crafts' or 'building crafts'. Whilst they were not intended to be vocational training courses, it was hoped that they might provide new incentives and interests. Back in school, integrated programmes coupling English, social and environmental studies and technical subjects were arranged. These were strongly vocationally biased, including a variety of industrial visits. High hopes have again been dashed by a lack of enthusiasm. Considerable absenteeism from the craft courses and industrial visits has been experienced. On one occasion, a particularly interesting industrial visit resulted in only four out of fourteen boys actually turning up at the plant. It has been difficult to find reasons for these features. One thing does seem clear however. The pupils seemed to feel that we were offering them something second class, which they resented, and therefore did not cooperate.

By contrast courses for older girls with a strong home-making bias have been much more successful. Many of the problems associated with older West Indian girls have largely disappeared, and difficult behaviour is now rare with fourth-year girls.

Other signs began to appear in 1967 and have developed progressively from then. These included many more difficulties with older West Indian boys. There were increases in truancy, stealing, conflicts within the family leading to the children leaving home, and more boys were coming before the courts. Classroom relationships with such groups deteriorated in many respects. We have found that general educational standards of West Indian children coming through primary schools are *not* improving as we had hoped, and that there is a serious level of disturbance among younger West Indian children, many of whom have been born in this country. There has been a deterioration in general atmosphere: this is reflected in noise, quarrelling and fighting amongst themselves; serious levels of pilfering, wanton damage to school property, equipment, books, etc. and generally disorderly conduct. On our side, we face a continuing lack of success in motivating children who have the ability to achieve much more than they do now.

Conditions have not improved and anxieties increased steadily over the past few years. Discussions with colleagues in similar schools indicate that the problem is a general one. More disturbing, some colleagues in primary schools with a similar pupil population suggest that the position is not likely to improve in the near future.

All these indications point to factors far deeper and of far greater complexity than had been realized. In hindsight one wonders why these were not appreciated earlier. In defence, however, it must be claimed that the sheer struggle for survival in the face of these enormously complex difficulties of the last ten years have scarcely allowed one to raise one's eyes above the immediate horizons or to detach oneself from the pressure of daily experiences to look objectively at the community around us and search for more fundamental causes. Further, there is little opportunity of real progression by experience, since staff changes occur with monotonous regularity, although it must be stressed that only a very small number of teachers have left because of our particular conditions. New teachers, including probationers, accept the challenge with encouraging cheerfulness, but each one has to learn by his own experience within the classroom situation. It would however be perhaps fair to say that there has been insufficient collective effort to discover and try to understand the basic underlying causes of difficulty.

Having reached a point of dissatisfaction with the situation as it was, I decided in 1968 to look for fresh sources of guidance and help. Approval was obtained to appoint a school counsellor: the post carried an additional head-of-department allowance and the counsellor would be additional to staffing ratio. I hoped to appoint a person with a special interest and knowledge of West Indian children and was fortunately able to meet this requirement. After her appointment, the counsellor, already trained and experienced, spent five months in the West Indies on a fact-finding tour, and returned to take up her appointment on 1 June 1969. A great deal of background work has now been done in a critical analysis of our structure, approaches, our aims and objectives. After several months of heart-searching, and at times painful, discussions, we came to certain conclusions, which will form the basis of considerable changes in our social and educational policy. They can be summarized as follows:

1. The major problem confronting the immigrant community as a whole in Handsworth is that of individual and group identity, and the great need in the schools is to counter the resulting lack of self-confidence which prevents many pupils from having any real concept of their latent abilities and strengths.

2. In the case of the West Indians, it is possible to trace the origins of this problem right back to slavery and the colonial history of the Caribbean; but in very many families their experiences in this country so far have substantially compounded their feelings of rejection and failure.

3. The difficulties exhibited and experienced by the children stem from a combination of many complex social, cultural and educational factors. The impact on the child is enormous and the school must provide an environment which will encourage active participation in social experiences of a positive nature; which will enable the pupils to share in decision-making and problem-solving; and which will create a situation where they will have opportunities to reveal themselves as individuals, often on an informal level, and develop a new realization of their own worth. Until each one sees this for himself, he cannot reveal it to others.

The effort of the school has to be geared to reinforcing this self-confidence among the children. Our teaching still tends to be too teacher centred and insufficiently pupil based for such a diverse school community.

Implicit therefore is an acceptance that the school environment and curricula must be geared to develop a 'pluralist' approach, recognizing and fostering worthwhile differences and giving individual groups an opportunity of development as groups whenever possible.

A new structure for pastoral care has been set up. Pastoral care, or form groups, are no longer the same as the teaching groups. The school has twenty form groups of approximately twenty-five pupils (excluding fifth year). Each form group consists of an age range of first to fourth year and a mixed ability range. A form period is timetabled daily from 9–9.40 a.m. This period will cover the following activities.

1. Form and pastoral-group work producing opportunities for participation.

2. House activities: five forms comprise a house. There is at present no formal school assembly. Assemblies, of varied style and approach, are being developed on a house basis, each group within the house contributing and it is hoped that assemblies will be pupil-based.

3. Establishment of a school council which meets weekly: providing further opportunties for responsibility, participation and decision-making.

4. The school counsellor will meet one house group of form tutors weekly so that each half-term there will have been at least one period of discussion with each group of tutors.

Great importance is attached to the part to be played by this period of our school day, since we hope it will help to create a feeling of greater security and stability in the children, without which real educational progress cannot be made.

Our two-band structure is also under review at the moment. As the numbers of West Indian pupils have increased, more have gone into the lower-band classes. It is mainly in these classes, which are often almost entirely composed of West Indian children, that the greatest difficulties are occurring. This perhaps is not surprising when we realize that these groups contain large proportions of pupils with similar emotional and social problems. Some way, therefore, has to be found to minimize this factor by arranging more balanced groups. Present indications are that we shall again depart from streaming or banding in the first three years. Classes will be unstreamed, but modified setting facilities will be retained. This we hope will reduce the adverse effects of concentrating pupils with problems too densely in a few classes.

Conclusions

Looking back it would be helpful perhaps to summarize the main changes which we have made over the past ten years. In the organization of teaching we have used strict streaming which we abandoned for mixed-ability groups; we then returned to a modified streaming or banding: now we have decided to revert to mixed-ability groups.

Secondly in trying to build a school community we are changing the pattern of form and house grouping to something similar to the primary school 'family group' structure. In these activities we are encouraging the children to develop a real sense of participation by creating opportunities for them to join in discussion and decision-making on many aspects of their school, house or form activities.

Finally we have abandoned the belief that it is sufficient to treat all children alike. This belief denied many of the children the opportunity to reveal skills or talents which would help them to feel a sense of success or achievement. As we now see it, the task of the school is to recognize, in much more positive ways than before, the group identity which the pupils have through their family history and their home culture. Indeed these factors are even more important in view of the position of immigrant pupils as a distinct minority group in their neighbourhood, city and in Britain generally. We now understand much more fully than ever before that a multi-racial school cannot succeed in either its educational or social aims if this is ignored. If any success is to be achieved in the community at large, success in the school community is vital.

5 Developing a Language Unit

Margaret Rogers

I was sent to the school to 'help the immigrant children with their English'. Just back in England after nine years overseas working in schools in Ghana and Kenya where English was the medium of instruction, but not the mother tongue of the learners, this seemed not too formidable an objective. The staff of the junior mixed and infants school were friendly and willing to be cooperative, but between us some effective organization needed to be developed. From my overseas experience I thought in terms of, perhaps, a beginners' group, an intermediate group and an advanced group. But it soon became clear that this kind of thinking was irrelevant in the situation of a multi-racial school in England. Indeed, my overseas experience needed a great deal of modification. Its irrelevance became brutally clear when I had 'tested' all the children of overseas parentage in the building. 'Tested' is too exact a term for the exercise. There were, and still are, no adequate tests developed to assess the things I needed to know. I decided that I needed to know:

1. Whether the child could communicate in the social situations of school, i.e. in the dining-room, answering personal questions, explaining reasons for behaviour, etc.

2. Whether the child could communicate in a learning situation (a) in an individual situation, (b) in a group situation, (c) in a class situation.

3. Whether the child could do both these things in all four of the language skills, (a) listening and understanding, (b) speaking and being understood, (c) reading and understanding, (d) writing and being understood.

It soon became obvious that the range of needs was extremely wide. The children fell roughly into three categories, those with little or no English, i.e. fairly recently arrived Greek, Turkish, Asian, Maltese, Italian, Chinese, etc.; those whose variant of English caused communication breakdowns in class (i.e. children from the Caribbean); and those who had 'picked up' some English, either in England or overseas, but which was quite inadequate for educational purposes. In the context of the day-to-day life of the school, the children in each of these categories need help.

In addition, the educational experiences of the children was varied, e.g. some eight year olds had little or no previous schooling; some ten year olds had schooling overseas in which they had become literate in their mother tongue in a script totally different from English, i.e. Urdu, Gujerati, etc. Also, a six year old learns in different ways from a ten year old whichever category he is in.

Another factor which was not part of my concern, but was very relevant to the school as a whole, was that many host community children in the school had severe learning difficulties. No rigid organization seemed viable to meet the range of needs, so it was agreed that a Language Unit would be developed. In the Junior Library and the adjoining store room cum corridor to the fire escape, it came into existence with two main aims: to teach English to those children throughout the school with little or no English; and to provide remedial and language development work for those in the upper age range whose inadequacy in English was handicapping their ability to participate fully in their normal classroom activities, and whose needs were urgent if they were to have a useful secondary school experience. The staff allocation was two full-time teachers and one welfare assistant.

The 'organization' must be flexible enough to absorb newcomers at any level. The teachers must also feel that they were receiving support. But how can this be achieved in a progressive primary school, with its integrated day, child-centred activity and discovery method approach? I spent some time in classes and tried to discover some of the language needs of the learners. Certainly my overseas experience of a 'graded structural' course needed wide modification.

In the class of six year olds who were building up block graphs in number work, the children needed to know the difference between 'all', 'most', 'some', 'a few', 'a lot', etc. – words their English counterparts used freely and accurately. No language-teaching materials reach these words in the beginning stages. The music and movement lessons on the radio used words like, 'reaching', 'sliding', 'twisting', 'turning', 'bending', 'find a space', 'make a circle', 'relax', etc. An infinite variety of contexts were used for these lessons ranging from the circus to traditional stories, all quite outside the experiences of most of the immigrant children.

However, it was for just these kinds of school situations that the immigrants, and their teachers, needed to be able to communicate.

The Language Unit, we therefore decided, must be a kind of workshop to provide the language tool needed for the class situation.

Of course it didn't, the task is too great, too little is known about classroom language, but we tried.

First, we prepared 'banks' of teaching materials around topics which seemed to crop up regularly at all levels of primary education, i.e. a kit on the seasons, Christmas, Guy Fawkes, colours, shapes, textures, etc. We made cut-outs for use on flannelgraphs, cellographs and later magnet boards, for the telling of traditional stories. To this we added 'language' games, tapes, worksheets and readers. We built up schemes for the social activities – stories acted out of the kinds of day-to-day episodes a child might encounter; a fall in the playground; a lost glove; dinner time; the school medical etc. We organized regular outings in connection with all our work – to the parks – journeys on buses and the underground, visits to the zoo, the country, the seaside.

In the Language Unit we were continually trying to provide more and more ways to help each individual child to learn at his own pace and in his own way, the language skill he needed at that particular time. To this end we used all the audiovisual aids we could get. Tapes and tape recorders, cine loops, language master machines. Film strips with linked tapes etc. The children became very skilful in operating the equipment by themselves. For each of these media we made original materials to meet the needs of our children. Our output was prodigious but we could never keep pace with the needs. We kept open doors to provide a language learning situation for anyone in need at any time of the day. Always the immigrant is in need of language *now*, not tomorrow, or next term. We learnt this painfully, and I still cannot see how this urgency of need can be met. It is so easy to see some things. The child who cannot establish possession verbally, who can't say 'It's mine', will use his fists or feet to communicate his rights. When he can't say 'He hit me' (and so is blamed for starting a fight in a language he doesn't understand well, but with actions he interprets clearly) then he becomes aggrieved. Any multi-racial school will have behaviour problems – the result of children reacting *normally* to what is for *them* an abnormal situation, but to say this does not offer solutions.

We found that the Language Unit needed to become a place where tensions could be relieved, where the 'talking' and activities were linked to the needs of the child: also, that the most effective learning was linked with 'doing'. Learning to talk in a new language means provision of situations for talk, more talk and always talk.

Let me give some examples. One year, Guy Fawkes Night was on a Friday. On the Monday before we mounted a programme for our beginners which, among other things, aimed to teach the warning language (and the *actions* that should follow); the vocabulary inherent in Bonfire Night; the traditional story; and incidentals like *1st, 2nd, 3rd, 4th, 5th, on Friday, tomorrow*, etc. On Monday we taught *firework*; *alight*; *he lit*; *bonfire*, etc., and told, with puppets and drawings, a story of a boy who was hurt in a firework accident.

On Tuesday we acted out the story and made a picture frieze (and learnt the 'warm' colours in the process). On Wednesday, we told the Guy Fawkes story and put it on to a tape – the children providing sound effects and crowd language. On Thursday we made a miniature bonfire in a sand tray. The warning language began to be used by the children and responded to by others. 'Don't touch', 'Stand back', 'It's alight', 'Be careful', etc. Of course safety-first ideas could be covered in such a situation – we 'smothered' the fire to put it out. Doing this later in the day with the more advanced group led to talk and work on the do's and don'ts of fire prevention in the home – a very essential lesson when so many oil heater fires occur in their multi-occupied houses. Their 'writing' activity was linked with the safety-first posters they made and put up around the school. But on Friday came the highlight of the week – the fireworks. I brought sparklers into school. We recapped the stories of the week and then everyone had some sparklers to light (over the sand tray, of course). This time, the excitement, fears, pleasures, loosened tongues and what came out was the language of the stories, the warnings, the pleasures, the requests and the comments likely to arise around any bonfire. A hectic morning, but it more than justified the efforts.

Our Welfare Assistant took the infants away to prepare for dinner and one or two of the older 'beginners' were helping to tidy the Language Unit, when the door burst open and all the infants were back. 'What's the matter?' I said. A Turkish girl acted as spokesman. 'We want to say Thank You.' She paused, then added 'We are very pleased with you.' (What a lot one learns from children; after this I was acutely aware of the number of times I said to a child 'That's good, I'm very pleased with you.')

Another completely different project related to the broadcasts being taken by one upper junior class. One series was on carpets, involving weaving, designing and a Persian story. For this we taught children how to do simple weaving (and so, of course, the relevant language) and to make patterns and designs; told the story simply with visual aids and finally wrote little reading cards about carpets and looms based on books which were in general use in the class. For those whose reading skill was limited we made tapes which 'talked' the book into the child's headset. In this way the class teacher was able to mount a class project around the broadcast in which everyone could become involved.

Our most successful work occurred when the whole school was involved in a school project. In 1966 we had a school project on 1066. Everyone in the building heard the story, and everyone was involved in a re-enacting of the episodes. In the Language Unit the recent arrivals learnt, *This is a sword/shield/tunic,* etc. At that time, it was more important to them than 'this is a pen/desk/book, etc. Tenses were related to the work in hand –

I'm making a sword, I've painted my helmet (so what shall I do now?), *I'm going to make a picture of a castle*, etc. We took children to see a castle (it's really a waterworks, but has all the features of a castle). They learnt, because they saw and used, *a moat, a drawbridge, a turret*. Back in school the beginners could make models, paintings, which they talked about. I taught some writing of stories leading to a climax in which I offered myself in situations of disaster – falling into the moat, locked up in the dungeon, shut up in the tower, etc. The comic-strip stories which developed out of this – with one of my 'disasters' as the final cartoon was not only a way of producing exciting writing in English – it was a tremendous release of tensions – to be able to laugh at and with authority! When a whole school project was in operation was the only time we really managed to keep abreast with making of teaching material. The whole of the learning fabric was one. What happened anywhere in the building had relevance. We could teach the appropriate vocabulary and patterns of English which the children heard and needed in all their classes.

This very flexible language workshop was the result of a combination of factors which are not always present – physical space – a large room and an annexe; a cooperative staff willing to experiment to meet the new situation; support from the head and the authority making equipment and personnel available.

None of the activities we used are exceptional in good primary classes. What we brought to these activities was an awareness of language and communication in English and a knowledge of language teaching and learning where English is the medium of instruction but *not* the mother tongue of the learner. Most teachers have not been trained in either of these skills.

Also, although there are texts related to language learning, there seem to be few, if any, texts related to subjects or projects which have been designed for primary-school learners in the English medium situation.

When the materials from the Schools Council Project at Leeds, SCOPE, were produced, together with SCOPE II for the development of reading and writing skills, it was possible to draw on these considerably for 'core' materials. The Schools

Council Project for West Indian Children will add to these resources.

Nevertheless, this is only the beginning. What made work in the Language Unit so exciting was the overlap into the individual classes and the integral part of our work with the school as a whole. One of our days of greatest pleasure was when some English children based some written work on one of our 'language' stories (it taught prepositions of movement in a subtle way through the thwarting of a bank robbery, e.g. 'he walked *past* the school *through* the park' etc.). One of our Greek children had taken his new 'book' to class and had read it there. Several children, English and other nationalities, produced other stories on the same pattern of language and brought them to us for duplicating, putting on tape, etc. and to add to our 'resource' bank. On that day we felt we were perhaps making a genuine contribution to multi-racial education.

All our efforts were still far from meeting the needs of the children and the teachers. We didn't know enough, we couldn't develop expertise and rationale quickly enough for the range of need. We would like to see the development of a rationale for the professional skills needed by all teachers in a multi-racial school. Because we have seen so many children leaving for secondary school already educationally and linguistically handicapped we worry about their futures; and, incidentally, about our society which needs so many people educated in ways that can keep pace with our technological development. For this we *all* need highly sophisticated skills in English, the tool of education. In the Language Unit we felt that we were beginning to evolve useful skills, of relevance to all those whose language skills are inadequate for the educational situations which are the norm of English schools.

6 Teaching English to Immigrants at a Secondary Girls School, 1964–1969

Doreen Manley

In 1964 I began to visit a Secondary Girls School in Sparkbrook, Birmingham, as a part-time English language teacher. I was one of a peripatetic team of teachers based in the LEA's Department of English as Second Language. During the subsequent five years the work I was able to do in this school developed in a particularly happy and interesting way, which has to a large extent provided me with a model of what can be achieved with a teacher from outside, in a school where educational needs are changing rapidly.

When I began there were about forty totally non-English speakers in my groups, the majority with no English at all. Some girls who could speak a little English were being helped by the remedial teachers. I had the use of two very small rooms (formerly a housecraft flat) and this meant limiting the number in each withdrawal group to ten girls. New girls, mainly Indian and Pakistani, were arriving in the school almost every week. Sometimes there would be ten newcomers in one week, usually with no knowledge of English, and frequently with no previous schooling. I began to spend more time at this school, and was soon giving half-hour lessons to eight groups of girls each day. This frequency of lessons was essential for beginners – one short lesson every day was much better than two long ones a week. In fact, a few girls who were unable to take part in normal classes stayed in the language groups for much of the school day during their first few months. New girls continued to arrive, and soon a majority of the school roll were from overseas – mainly from India, Pakistan and the Caribbean.

Because of the pressure of new arrivals, I often had to drop the best girls from my groups, even when they could still benefit from extra help. However, most of these children continued to make good progress, because of their own efforts, and the efforts of the staff. Subject teachers worked hard to adapt their teaching methods to the changed school situation, and to teach English at the same time as their specialist subjects. I was readily accepted by the staff and was frequently asked for help and advice.

I taught by the direct method, following closely a fairly rigid syllabus of my own, broadening out gradually in an ever widening series of structures and sentence patterns, and teaching the girls to understand and use all the tenses. Although some sections of textbooks and materials which had been produced for overseas were useful, most of the materials were unsatisfactory for two reasons: they were not geared to life in Britain nor to the language required in English schools. I found it necessary to make a good deal of the reading and writing materials myself and prepared tapes and apparatus for individual and small group-work.

There were plenty of formal language-teaching sessions, followed up by various activities: handwork, language games, reading and writing, outings and visits to places nearby, all serving to practise the language learned in the formal periods. The visits also broadened the girls' experiences of English life. These excursions were often the only time some of the girls went out, and they gave me an invaluable chance to get to know the girls as individuals, not just pupils in a class.

In September 1967, my class was one of the trial classes for the Schools Council Project in English for immigrant children. Although most of the ideas and work suggested there were very close to what I had already been doing, it was marvellous to have a syllabus to work from, and the visuals, work cards and books to use. As soon as the SCOPE* materials were produced, we bought them and I have been using them with increasing enthusiasm ever since.

While the intake of immigrants increased, the overall numbers of the children attending the school dropped, and in 1967 I was able to move into a large, well-equipped, classroom, and usually taught much larger groups of girls, twenty to thirty at a time. I kept them for longer lessons, and now spent three and a half days

* SCOPE: an introductory English course for immigrant children: Stage I, Books for Schools Ltd for the Schools Council, 1969.

at the school. There were fewer newcomers, and I had a chance to give more help with reading and writing.

One major problem which has to be faced by every language teacher is how to give sufficient practice, sufficient talking time, to each pupil in such large groups. Children learn to talk by talking. Each girl needed time to practise aloud what she had learned in oral lessons. It was no use to merely understand, and go through a syllabus once, they had to *practise* spoken English, until the language became a familiar part of themselves, ready to be used easily in real-life situations.

I decided that, for the girls to get maximum talking practice, they should work in twos. So, most of the language work learned in the oral lessons was practised again in pairs, the most popular way in the form of dialogues. I found many advantages in this: every child had maximum talking-practice time, friends enjoyed working together, and it was good preparation for later dialogue work, and drama in small groups. At first we used no typed text or reading matter. I simply taught the relevant structure myself. For example, I put a penny on the table, and taught, 'The penny's on the table. It's on the table.' I then asked 'Where's the penny?' and got the response, 'It's on the table.' After a few class lessons on the prepositions, the children were ready to practise, in pairs. One girl put a penny on the table, or in a box, or under the blackboard, etc., and asked her friend, 'Where's the penny?' and got the correct answer. The children moved about the room, of course. This involved all twenty or so girls talking at once, but somehow we managed to do it reasonably quietly. In the early stages, simple instructions like, 'Stop, listen to me', and so on, were vitally important, to avoid chaos!

In one lesson, I taught, 'next to, in front of, behind' ('I'm sitting next to Rovia', 'She's sitting behind Anna', etc). Practice in twos followed. These are examples of the 'talk' practice that went on all over the classroom.

PUPIL 1: Where are you sitting?
PUPIL 2: I am sitting *next to* Zehra.

PUPIL 1: Where are you sitting?

PUPIL 2: I'm sitting *in front of* Rifat.

then:

PUPIL 1: Where is Rovia sitting?
PUPIL 2: She's sitting *next to* Anna.

then:

PUPIL 1: Who's sitting *behind* Anjana?
PUPIL 2: Rovia is.

It was easy to teach 'Nobody':

PUPIL 1: Who's sitting behind Anna?
PUPIL 2: Nobody.

I taught the future tense, which uses 'going to'.
e.g. 'I'm going to wash the floor.'
    'She's going to clean the windows.'
I then drew a house on the board, step by step, and asked the class
'What am I going to draw next?' At each point they guessed,
'You're going to draw a door', 'You're going to draw a window',
etc. This, again, they practised in pairs, with one girl drawing and
asking, 'What am I going to draw next?' and the other guessing
and answering.

Of course, drawing and guessing was equally useful for teaching
the present perfect tense, e.g.

PUPIL 1: What have you drawn?
PUPIL 2: I've drawn a tree.

All this oral practice in twos was done without any text, but with
the girls copying my speech sounds and intonation as exactly as
possible.

Oral practice in twos led naturally on into more complex
dialogue work. Sometimes I wrote the dialogues on the board,
sometimes had them typed and duplicated. I relied heavily on
Dr Michael West's work *Easy English Dialogues*. As he had
never had the opportunity to use these as he wished, he asked me to
cooperate with him in a year's experiment, to write and use
dialogues with immigrants learning English. I kept records of the
full year's work and we were both reasonably pleased at the end
of it by the girls' confidence in spoken English.

I wrote the dialogues under two headings: 'Friends Talking' – the sort of conversations friends might hold, and 'School Dialogues', which practised the language useful in a school situation. The dialogues were based on real-life situations which I had observed. They were not to be found in any of the normal textbooks. The language of the dialogue was not completely new to the girls, as many terms had already been learned in a language lesson.

This was our usual procedure. I would speak the dialogue, and explain it often with gestures and actions. The children then repeated the dialogue after me, line by line, copying my intonation as exactly as possible. The whole class then practised the dialogue in twos, looking at the text when necessary, and then learned it by heart. I circulated among them, listening and correcting. Then I asked certain pairs of girls to speak the dialogue to the whole class. When the dialogue was known, I asked the girls to substitute other words and phrases for certain ones in the text, suggesting substitutes at first. The children soon invented their own versions without changing the correct pattern of the dialogue.

Some examples will clarify:

MR JONES: Do you want a dinner at school today, Abdul?
ABDUL: No, thank you. I don't want a school dinner today.
MR JONES: Are you going home for dinner?
ABDUL: Yes, I am.

MR JONES: Why were you away from school yesterday?
ABDUL: I had a bad cold.
MR JONES: Are you better now?
ABDUL: Yes, thank you.

For 'I had a bad cold', the girls substituted: 'I had a bad cough', 'I had a sore throat', 'I had a toothache', etc.

ABDUL: Mr Jones, I've lost my coat.
MR JONES: Have you looked in the cloakroom?
ABDUL: Yes, I have.
MR JONES: Here it is. It's on this chair.
ABDUL: Thank you.
'My coat' was changed to 'my anorak', 'my mac', 'my pullover', and so on.

One dialogue dealt with 'borrow' and 'lend':

PUPIL 1: May I borrow your pencil, please?
PUPIL 2: Certainly. Here it is.
PUPIL 1: Oh, dear. I haven't got my ruler, either.
PUPIL 2: It's all right. I'll lend you my ruler.
PUPIL 1: Thank you very much.
PUPIL 2: Not at all.

We did the simple present ('Where does your father work?' etc.) and useful past forms, like *went, bought*. We practised polite conversations for visitors:

PUPIL 1: Hallo! Do come in!
PUPIL 2: Thank you.
PUPIL 1: Do sit down. Have a chair by the fire. Would you like a cup of tea?
PUPIL 2: No, thank you. I don't drink tea.
PUPIL 1: Would you like a cup of coffee, then?
PUPIL 2: Yes, please.

'I used to' is common in speech, but difficult for the learner.

PUPIL 1: I'm working very hard at school now.
PUPIL 2: So am I.
PUPIL 1: I used to paint pictures in the evening. I'm too busy now.
PUPIL 2: Yes. I used to watch television every evening but I don't have time now, I have too much homework.

'I've got to' is another common pattern.

PUPIL 1: Can you come out tonight?
PUPIL 2: No, I'm afraid not.
PUPIL 1: Oh, why not?
PUPIL 2: I've got to stay at home.
PUPIL 1: Why?
PUPIL 2: I've got to help my father.

'Help my father' changed to 'help my mother', 'wash my hair', 'do my homework', 'go to the launderette'.

Practice of these dialogues helped all the girls to gain the confidence and fluency they needed in order to take a full part in school life and to talk to their English friends.

This work led on naturally to longer dialogues, or short plays. The plays were based on home or school situations, or short folk and traditional stories. I wrote and duplicated the scripts. All the girls practised at once, in small groups of twos, or threes, or fours. The girls first acted the plays with the script, then without, then added their own dialogue. The additions were usually in correct English, as they had a firm base to build on. The home 'situations' were based on shopping incidents, visits, TV breakdown, accidents in the home, getting up on a cold morning, etc. Sometimes we adapted a folk story and combined it with a home theme. An adaption of the story *There's a bear in my bed*, with the situation of everybody working on jobs in the house, went like this:

There's a bear in my bed

PETER: Mummy. There's a bear in my bed!

MOTHER: Go away, Peter. I'm busy. I'm sweeping the floor.

PETER: Daddy. There's a bear in my bed!

FATHER: Go away, Peter. I'm busy. I'm painting the door.

PETER: Tony. There's a bear in my bed!

TONY: Go away, Peter. I'm busy. I'm doing my homework.

PETER: Ann. There's a bear in my bed!

ANN: Go away, Peter. I'm busy. I'm making a frock.

ZOO-KEEPER: Has anybody seen a bear? It's escaped from the zoo.

PETER: A bear? Yes. I've seen a bear. It's asleep on my bed.

MOTHER: Peter, why didn't you tell me?

FATHER: Peter, why didn't you tell me?

TONY: A bear?

ANN: I'm frightened.

PETER: I told you all. I said, 'There's a bear in my bed', but you were all too busy. Listen to me next time.

ZOO-KEEPER: I'll get the bear now, and take it to the zoo.

When the girls had practised several times, they changed the play by substituting other actions and sentences for the lines after 'I'm busy', e.g.

MOTHER: I'm busy. I'm cleaning the windows.

As the girls' knowledge of the spoken language increased, they were able to use drama more and more. Sometimes they divided into groups and made up their own themes – losing money was a popular one.

Sometimes I read a story, using explanations and pictures to make the action understood. On the second reading the class joined in while I was reading, sometimes making sound effects such as the wind or sea, or a crowd, later improvising some dialogues for the characters. Finally the girls divided into groups and acted out the story.

They all neeeded to learn to read English. For most of the girls, this was their first experience of learning to read and write. I borrowed a number of early readers from the local infant and junior schools. These were not really suitable for the older girls but they were so anxious to learn to read that the books were well used. To take a book home was considered very important. Also, I made use of the Public Libraries' Teachers' Borrowing Scheme. Each term I borrowed a large selection of well produced, attractive books, in simple English, both fiction and non-fiction, which we could not afford in school.* At least one session a week was spent in the girls choosing a book and reading it for pleasure. Many of them lived in crowded home conditions, and the chances of reading quietly at home were few, so they enjoyed a peaceful session when they could get deeply involved in a good book, without interruption. It was not always easy to find suitable books, because books for English children often use forms and structures too advanced for children learning English as a second language. However, many were very suitable, and I was fortunate to have the valuable assistance of the deputy children's librarian. We decided to make an exhibition of these books, and others useful to immigrants and their teachers, at the Language Centre Hockley, in April 1970. I hope this kind of exhibition can be made available in various schools for parents.

How did the girls get on in their specialist subjects and how did the school generally fare as the proportion of immigrant girls rose? The school had held a good record for steady work and behaviour in the community, and this continued, despite the more difficult circumstances.

*e.g. The Read for Fun Series, The Zozo Series and The World's Work Series.

The relationship between staff and girls was a friendly and happy one, and no newcomer felt lost, as she was quickly accepted and known well by certain of the teachers. The girls felt secure in the knowledge that the teachers genuinely cared about their interests and their educational achievements. Meanwhile I worked very closely with a number of the ordinary subject teachers.

The needlework teachers soon discovered that every process in needlework had to be demonstrated and explained in simple English at the same time. 'It's a pattern', 'It's a hem', 'I'm sewing with small stitches', etc. In this way, learning to sew and learning the English language used in the sewing process went naturally together. Of course, much more individual help was necessary than formerly. But the work produced was excellent, both in craft and garment work, and a fashion show was a part of many parents' evenings.

The music staff continued to keep music making as a popular part of school life. However, during my last year there, the presence of twenty-five non-English speakers in the first year 'C' stream made singing lessons very difficult. The girls lacked experience of English music and reading ability, but not enthusiasm. The music teacher and I made a collection of simple folk songs, in easy language, often with plenty of repetition. Songs like *Little Red Wagon, Old MacDonald, Skip to my Lou* and *Fair Rosie* were very popular. We made a little duplicated book of songs, then we worked together teaching the girls to read and sing the songs, she in music and I in the English lessons. The girls also took the books home to learn the words. Some songs are included in the SCOPE materials and we made a songbook of these also.

I also cooperated with the domestic-science teacher. She would give me the recipe and list of ingredients early each week, so that I could help the girls to buy them, and to explain, for instance, the different kinds of sugar she asked them to buy: granulated, castor, brown, demerara, icing. We went shopping together for the ingredients and our dialogues were practised in a real-life situation.

Then, during the actual lesson, as the teacher demonstrated, she said what she was doing – 'I'm beating the fat', 'I'm adding the flour', 'I'm breaking an egg', so that the meanings of the cookery verbs were clear. After the cookery lesson, in an English period with me, the girls would frequently act out the whole previous lesson in small groups. One girl in each group would be the teacher, and give directions and help the others, while they mimed the lesson.

The art teacher infected the children with his own enthusiasm for painting, frequently painting with the children. As he painted, he talked simply and demonstrated clearly. At the end of an art session I was often invited to help to extend conversation activity related to the work the girls produced. Some of the girls enjoyed this so much they continued to paint as a leisure activity. The work produced at the school was quite exceptional, and much of it was shown in exhibition.

The importance of this joint work was that I was not isolated, and the pupils could clearly link their language work to the rest of their school life. Awareness of their educational needs extended throughout the school.

The deputy head had been a very skilled teacher of English to the upper forms in the past; realizing the needs of the changed situation, she took a year's course in English as a Second Language, gaining the RSA teacher's certificate, so was very competent to help the progress of the immigrants' English in the more advanced, as well as beginner, stages. The school was also most fortunate in its head teacher, who was extremely supportive both to her staff and to the pupils. The girls felt secure in her genuine interest and approval.

It is difficult in retrospect to pinpoint exactly what the special strength of this school was, when other apparently similar schools seemed overwhelmed by difficulties. I believe it lay partly in the fact that the curriculum aims were based on reality, and partly in that the staff realized that learning English was a priority, and that subject learning and English had to go hand in hand. All teachers were prepared to think anew about the language of their subject and cooperation between the staff was high. Above all, there was a great deal of hard work put into dealing with the new situation, and a ready acceptance of the newcomers as persons, which led to the positive and friendly relationships throughout the school. A stable staffing situation helped to ensure continuity and a tradition emerged relevant to the multi-racial character of the school.

7 Social Studies for a Multi-Racial Society

Margaret Nandy

There is a sense in which every school in Britain is multi-racial. Whether or not our multi-racialism is reflected in the school population, every child in every school is going to be an adult in a multi-racial society. Although most schools and teachers are not faced with the urgency to create a curriculum which will have some impact on their pupils' thinking on race relations, the reason for doing this applies in every school. Changes are long overdue, particularly in the teaching of colonial history, and the development of courses broadly in the social-studies field, which will enable pupils to acquire tolerant attitudes to people of different races and nationalities, whether they are living in Britain or throughout the rest of the world. In fact it is only because there are now coloured children in our classes, that teachers have had their eyes focused on an area of study which has been in need of change for many years. Suddenly, we have been made aware that the most readily available materials on, for example, the Age of Exploration, on slavery, on colonialism, are embarrassingly ethnocentric, and aware too that the teacher's traditional attitude of studied impartiality when 'hot' issues come under discussion is inadequate, and in fact potentially damaging when race relations is the issue.

Race relations is, of course, only one of many 'crisis issues' which teachers are beginning to see as their legitimate concern. One reason for their increasing interest is because for the first time society's 'problem members' do not all leave school at fifteen; nor do they all congregate at the lower end of the most neglected secondary modern. Most urban schools have coloured pupils and the inadequacy of education in race relations is plain; but most secondary schools too have amongst their pupils drug takers, the sexually experienced, members of skinhead gangs, despite the fact that teachers often convince themselves that these all attend the school down the road. Their presence has contributed to an unprecedented growth in social science teaching. In my view the whole of social science or social studies teaching presents problems to teachers in the same way in which the exaggerated case of race relations does. The central problem seems to me to be this: we want to impart knowledge not for its own sake, but to contribute to the formation of a rational viewpoint in our pupils; but our objective is thwarted by the personal involvement of the pupils, and their tenacious predisposition to a viewpoint they have already acquired by non-rational means. It is in the general context of social-science teaching that I see education for a multi-racial society, and race-relations goals formed only part of the project which we devised.

The two Leicestershire schools in which I have been working are an eleven to fourteen and an eleven to eighteen comprehensive. In both schools there is a wide range of ability, and the social-class composition is predominantly skilled working class. In both schools, the basic organization is not streamed, and in neither is there any attempt to grade children academically in their social science work. In common with most multi-racial schools (schools who have some minority group pupils) they are overwhelmingly English schools – their character has not really been altered by the presence of children from the Commonwealth. They have not felt the pressures which have inspired some schools to change their curriculum in order to take more account of different nationalities and cultures.

We began by examining existing types of social science courses, to see if, in isolating the reasons for their inadequacy, we could begin to specify the essentials of a course that would achieve something really worthwhile. There has been a tremendous growth of social science courses in schools recently, bearing all the marks of a panic response to an unexpected demand. The vogue for exposing social problems in the mass media has intensified the sense of urgency and the result has been a mushrooming of *ad hoc* courses to fill the gap. There seem to be two main types of stop-gap courses, neither of which appears to be capable of enlarging children's perception of the social environment, but both of which certainly cause the frustration which many teachers feel at beating their heads against the impenetrable apathy and insensitivity of their pupils. The first type of course I call *cataloguing institutions*. We are now all too familiar with textbooks available for schools whose chapter headings go something like this: the individual, the family, the home, the school, industry, government, justice, religion.

The implicit justification for such a course is that pupils will 'bank' the information provided and will emerge with a total picture of their society. In our view this seemed optimistic and unproven: it was just as likely that pupils would look on this knowledge as bits of information unrelated to their real concerns or interests. It might well end up, that is, not as a bank from which they draw, but as a rubbish dump! Courses of this kind fail in two ways. First, they fail to provide the analytical tools which are essential if pupils are to build up a coherent picture of society as a whole, in which the relationships between the institutions, culture and individuals make some kind of pattern. Secondly, it provides no way in which pupils can evaluate the institutions they are learning about – in other words, no comparative perspective. The second type of course I call '*social problem spotting*'. The chapter headings are familiar too: war, race, drugs, poverty, strikes. . . . The rationale of this kind of course is that by giving the child the opportunity to discuss these topics he is enabled to form his own viewpoint. In fact, the typical response is quite different. The pupil starts with a hazy knowledge of the subject, but is unwilling to accept the fact that his knowledge is incomplete, because the subjects are so familiar to him – he is likely to have heard them discussed on television, for example. He expresses his viewpoint, rejects any information that does not fit into that viewpoint, and leaves the class with his views probably reinforced because he has had to articulate them in public.

Once a public stance of this sort is taken up, no amount of information or evidence will transform what is essentially a prejudiced viewpoint into a rational one. What is wrong in both types of courses is that they provide no training in the logic of forming a point of view after looking at the facts and of altering a point of view in the light of new evidence. The whole process of forming conclusions in the light of factual evidence is missing. Teaching this process must be the first priority of social studies courses.

I think it is important to remind ourselves frequently that to most children there is nothing self-evident about the moves between evidence and conclusions. There is no intrinsic reason why facts should be more convincing to him than, say, loyalty to parents or friends, in fact very much the opposite is often the case. We need to be aware that unreasoned action is not the same as irrational action. Loyalty is often, for adults as well as children, a much more important social attribute than the ability to stand apart and reason. In a strike, a gang fight, an election campaign, in love relationships, loyalty is vital. We cannot, and should not try to, supplant it. But we can make pupils more rationally aware of it, and try to provide some understanding of the occasions when it is inappropriate or harmful, when personal integrity should come first. We can only hope to succeed in this when our pupils have learned to have confidence in their own powers of analysis and reasoning, their own judgement. As teachers we are, of course, committed to rational decision-making, but so often we forget how artificial it is for most school children.

I am emphasizing this point because it is obviously very important for teachers attempting to improve race relations. We know from studies like the PEP Report* that appeals to group loyalty are frequently made to try and justify racial discrimination ('what would the neighbours/employees think?'); in the ugliest incidents of race hatred and violence, group loyalty becomes the loyalty to pack, or lynch mob; the issue of how far anyone can differ from his peer group also arises in multi-racial classrooms when minority pupils are baited, or more often ostracized, by the majority. What I would argue is that the individual teacher cannot hope to do much about this kind of situation by providing more *knowledge* unless the general curriculum of the school is geared to building up open-minded and reasoning attitudes in pupils, and giving them confidence in their own reasoning powers.

I think it fair to say that the two models of social studies courses dominate social science teaching in secondary schools today. Their objectives – to facilitate a comprehension of society, its problems, its direction, its potentiality for change and the

* See W. W. Daniel, *Racial Discrimination in England*, Penguin, 1966.

leeway of the individual in it – are indeed honourable. The trouble is that their approach is self-defeating. This is because the material used in such courses – material drawn from the children's own society and time – is too emotionally charged to be examined with detachment, too complex to exhibit patterns readily, too familiar to ask fundamental questions about. We cannot automatically expect children to find the structure and function of sundry assorted institutions interesting if they take them as given, as fixed landmarks. It is only when they have acquired an awareness that things could be differently ordered that they can be led to ask why things are ordered in this particular way, and whether that way is efficient, desirable, humane and so on. The final defect of the typical social studies courses is that they usually begin so late. Any serious attempt at education in this field must start early enough to teach methods of approach and to build up understanding of the essential concepts which pupils will need to examine the society in which they live.

At least three points emerge from this examination of the inadequacies of our present typical courses. First, the value of starting social science teaching with a younger age group than is normally the case – in fact, the younger, the better. Ideally I think this should start in primary school. Already a great deal of unconscious social education goes on there, through drama, play in wendy houses, and so on. But it is usually unconscious because there is no follow-up discussion and writing about social relationships deliberately fostered by the teacher. So the effect of such play and drama is only to make more explicit the existing knowledge which children have of their world, and it is not used to open up the possibility of considering other structures. I am not suggesting that primary-school teachers should labour this, but simply that they should give these essentially useful play activities the same serious thought which is given to 'work' which begins, e.g. at playing shops, and is used to create a learning situation about money and number. At the secondary stage, it is sometimes thought that sociological material will be dull at the age when children's natural enthusiasm is the teacher's main source of success. In fact, I used anthropological material and found that here was a wealth of material which fascinated the eleven and twelve year olds I was teaching. It was ideal for use as a base from which the children could begin to make tentative hypotheses about the nature of human social relationships. There is a vast collection of traditional history and geography material, already familiar to teachers, which only needs rearranging to emphasize the human behaviour content in order to become immediately useful.

Secondly, there has to be a leisurely rate of progress. There needs to be time for the child to sufficiently ponder over the whole subject, so that he can possess the results of his study inwardly and can draw on it as working capital in the future. Experimental research has shown us that knowledge of 'facts', however interestingly they may be presented, is usually short-lived and rarely enables children to make generalizations within a subject. One reason is surely that we have been trying to teach too much in social science. The current trend away from traditional GCE courses and towards an increasing element of individual project work is an attempt to teach less, but to make an individual impact on the pupils' own thinking. In our approach, we were concerned to test not how much information the children had remembered, but the kind of thinking they learned from the materials we and they provided. But an approach of this kind, where children are not under pressure to rote-learn, but are pursuing a theme for its own intrinsic interest to them, needs time.

Thirdly, an effective teaching approach requires a huge bank of materials. Fortunately there is more and more suitable printed material coming on to the market, and more collections of documents and projects kits are being produced commercially. However, there is certainly never enough material available from these sources either to completely stock a whole course, or to satisfy the individual requirements of each school's courses. We found that there had to be a personal commitment on the part of all the staff involved in our social studies course: we had to be prepared and able to make slides, make film, record programmes, write texts, annotate standard texts, and so on. The work involved seemed overwhelming sometimes, and could not have been done if it had not been planned by a team of teachers. This kind of effort highlights the critical lack of technical assistance in most schools.

We realized from the start that how children acquired sociological material would be of crucial importance – because on this would depend to a large extent how they handled the material, and how they used it to arrive at a point of view. It was obviously necessary to establish a pattern of inquiry, followed by discussion and conclusions, and to encourage constant criticism of statements which could not be substantiated. The process of inquiry throws a great burden on teachers and there is a great deal of intrinsic value in children being left to find out information themselves, because there will come a time when this is the only method available to them. But there are drawbacks. As you watch children in the lower secondary school doing this you cannot fail to note that it is in many ways an inefficient way of proceeding and provides too many potential digressions from the real objective of the exercise. Children can go into the library to find out something quite specific and return with something related but different; or they can find a problem too hard and scale it down; or they can spend hours collecting data for its own sake and retain very little of it. Of course library resources must be made available, but I do not think anything is lost educationally if teachers sometimes provide children with the essential and relevant information directly.

In two years of teaching some anthropology to first-year pupils I was able to compare the results of the two methods of acquiring information. In the first year the children were largely dependent on library books for information about a hunting society. The results of their researches looked good, but they retained only a small proportion of the information they had gathered. It was therefore difficult to proceed to the original objective of the course – a discussion of the rationale of such societies. In the second year, the introduction to the course was provided for them – it was, in fact, a brilliant anthropological film.* It led to first-class discussion and further inquiry, and was still vividly remembered after six months. There are clearly many ways in which teachers can vary their methods at the inquiry stage.

But whatever method of information collection, it is only a preliminary to the essential work of evaluation. We had to find ways in which children could begin to find answers to questions

* *The Hunters*, filmed in the Kalahari by the Marshall Thomas team available from the Contemporary Films.

like 'what does this tell me about Man?' In another class where the basic theme concerned ancient history, the children used materials about Roman society to investigate the concept of 'civilization'. They started with formulations like 'cleaner', 'better houses', and so on. But because some of the children emphasized aspects of Roman society like slavery, while others were concerned with mosaics and baths, their initial formulations evolved into a discussion of the question 'better for whom?'. They produced quite a sophisticated debate on whether Roman society had on the whole done anything for anyone who was not a freeman. They had started with a hazy and undifferentiated notion of 'civilization' as in general an approved thing, and had come to appreciate the much more complicated notion that a state of affairs (like 'civilization') which produced welfare for some could also produce diswelfare for others.

At the very beginning of our social studies course, however, the most important objective was to enable the children to grasp some of the basic aspects of human life – its social character, the abilities which are unique to man, the fact that there is a logic to all patterns of human social development. We found the necessary materials to provide a comparative perspective initially in studies of animal organization, and later in anthropology. The eleven year olds spend six to eight weeks right at the start of their secondary schooling with materials about animal social organization, birds, insects, fish, primates. Of course at this stage there are incidental objectives: the complex business of getting used to a library, training to use the printed word as rather more than a copy book, training to use tape-recorders and slide projectors, experience in organizing groups for discussion. So perhaps the two main academic achievements of this stage of the project are an assorted accumulation of facts about animal behaviour, and a vague realization that there is something different about 'our cat claws the door to say that she wants to go out' and human communication. The notion that 'they're just like humans' takes a knock. It is at this stage, when it can be assumed that most of the children will feel some confidence in our 'peculiar' methods of work, that we turn to anthropology, on which they spend about ten weeks using much more structured material. My own fascination is in the Bushmen of the Kalahari because their organization is on a small enough scale for children to make their first attempts to grasp some of the fundamental prerequisites of human organization. But material about Eskimos, Australian Aborigines or any other hunting–gathering group would be equally suitable. Towards the end of the period of work the pupils are encouraged to make cross-cultural comparisons, and to re-examine their ideas of Stone Age man in Europe in the light of their new knowledge.

At the end of this part of the course, the majority of children are no longer satisfied with simplistic (and derisory) answers such as 'they build houses like this because they are stupid'. We looked, for example, at the question of what a Bushman would do if rehoused in a new council house, and the pupils were able to argue that such a house would be an encumbrance if one's way of life involved constant travel, and would be abandoned. Detailed testing of the effect of such work on children's thinking is not easy. It is clear from discussions, from recorded work and from their writing that they learn a great deal about the *fact* of Bushman society – but this is not the point of the course. I devised two kinds of test to attempt to find out about the development of the children's thoughts about that society. One test involved children making choices between pairs of statements, for example, between 'Bushmen don't write because they don't need to' and 'Bushmen don't write because they are unintelligent'. To my surprise, when I used this as a pre-test the children scored incredibly highly. I could only explain this as a reflection of their views of me, that I was unlikely to spend my time being interested in a group of people who were unintelligent, greedy, selfish, etc. The second type of test, an open-ended one, I found more helpful. The same questions, e.g. 'Bushmen do not write because . . .' is left for the children to complete. It is then scored on a positive, negative and neutral scale, and administered before and after the unit of work. In general I found that when asked particular questions to test the degree to which they had internalized the logic of the totally different society, they produced startlingly sophisticated reasoning. What is more, they had implicitly accepted the notion that no human culture can be regarded as a curio or as a demonstration of the right or wrong way to do things, but they had seen that another society, quite different from their own, could work for its members, provide physical and emotional security and provide a code of right and wrong. This provided an invaluable basis from which to begin future work which involved material drawn from Indian and West Indian cultures, and some of the common preconceptions and prejudices had already been countered.

In the complete five-year course as now planned, contemporary British society and race relations in Britain are not included explicitly until the fourth and fifth years. Of course, comparative work leads children to use material from their own society, and in discussion these fields are not avoided, but the lead-up to more intensive study of them continues in the second and third years. In both years, the children will make a thorough going study of another society's culture. In year two, we have chosen the Indian subcontinent, and in year three, America. But although better race relations is only one of the aims of the whole course, we have, even in the lead-up period, quite clear objectives. For example, in the study of other cultures we are quite clear about attempting to build up a sympathetic appreciation of them, to delay hostile judgements, and make it harder for pupils to come to oversimplified conclusions. In the study of India and America, the materials are designed to immerse the pupils as fully as possible in the total culture, not only its geography and history. I believe this is essential if we are to avoid the possible worsening of the pupils' attitudes to the peoples they encounter. (In standard geography texts the student learns that the Indian peasant uses very out-of-date methods of farming, and learns little else. He cannot be blamed for concluding that the Indians he meets are likely to be simple-minded. From his studies of Indian history, or more rightly, the history of the British in India, he is likely to feel that the Indians had no culture, and that the arrival of British colonialism was an unmixed benefit.) If we are to do anything to improve race relations through social studies work, the pupils must be given enough varied material to begin to understand the complexities of Indian society, to contemplate its cultural and historical achievements and to understand its contemporary problems. This kind of appreciation, understanding, of the society from which one of Britain's minorities has come, can be triggered to some use in future discussion of race relations as such. It is also an attempt to show the English pupil the Indian pupil in a new light – not as an immigrant, but as a person with a cultural identity.

The materials which we use as background to immigration from the West Indies are in two parts: a unit in the second year which focuses largely on developments in Africa before European exploration and up to the period of liberation; and a unit in the third year on America. Again, pupils' usual encounters with Africa at school are confined to the slave trade and the Boer Wars. The usual teaching methods encourage the view (often shared by West Indian pupils) that Africans were indeed lucky to be rescued from savagery! One of the problems faced by black youngsters is that their formal education here and in the West Indies and America has done nothing so far to challenge this view, and is one cause of the phenomena of self-hate. The reaction away from this has produced a growing demand for so-called Black Studies, a demand which urgently needs to be met. Reviewing the materials available, one finds that the best is very much orientated towards the British view, and this is not good enough. At best, they might engender pity for the slave, who is seen through the eyes of the nineteenth-century liberal reformers. Our problem was to get beyond pity, to respect for the person. We tried to do this by virtually rewriting all the material to stress the culture of Africa, the reasons within African society which allowed enslavement to take place, its effects in Africa, and we have put much more stress on African liberation movements and the slave rebellions than is usually the case. We attempt to give both black and white pupils some idea of Negro history to develop respect for self or respect for others which is the crucial missing factor in contemporary race relations.

The whole course is meant to serve a two-fold purpose. It is intended to provide the comparative material whch is the essential perspective giving information necessary to a study of contemporary society. And it is also intended to provide the essential background to an intelligent study of race, in a way which does not call forth the pupils' prejudices and fears, effectively stopping all learning. Research indicates that provision of knowledge to counteract prejudice has little impact; I would describe our approach to social studies as an attempt to *forestall* prejudice. It, too, may be a failure, but it is certainly worth attempting. It is, in fact, a way of providing black, brown and white studies for all children, black, brown and white; to try to cultivate conscious knowledge and respect of people who are different, something which we felt was dangerously lacking in race relations in many schools.

8 Race in the Curriculum

Hugh Cunningham

This is about my experience in a school in the Midlands and my later thinking on what was attempted, where we were successful, and where we were not. Inevitably, therefore, this is not a surefire recipe of a successful curriculum to achieve racial tolerance, but rather an attempt to consider what can be done within the existing curriculum and what changes in approach are needed as I see them.

The school was a modern school of 750 pupils, many of whom came from immigrant families from Central Europe. However, despite this and the thriving cultural activities of some of these communities, we did not see ourselves as a multi-racial school. Immigrants and race became a 'problem' with the sudden increase of coloured pupils; within eighteen months numbers leapt from a dozen comfortably integrated pupils to close on two hundred. And many of these had severe learning difficulties, either non-English speakers or Asian and West Indian pupils from rural areas with little regular education.

The account of what we did to meet this challenge is not offered as a piece of successful practice (I am sure many schools did better) but because it shows the questions we did not ask, because we did not even see them, about the organization and curriculum of a multi-racial school.

Initially we concentrated upon two problems; indeed they appeared so threatening, it was only later possible to realize that they had forced us to pay attention to weaknesses that existed before the arrival of coloured pupils. This is true of much that happened, both in the teaching and the organization. The needs of coloured immigrant pupils are not divorced from those of all pupils, and therefore measures to deal with their specific needs inevitably have implications for the whole curriculum and organization of the secondary school.

The first problem was the language difficulty of non-English-speaking pupils from Asian countries. What was happening was that they were congregating in the lower, so-called remedial classes. But as the numbers increased in these classes, so it became a travesty to call them remedial classes. The remedial department was disappearing under the pressure of numbers of non-English speakers, and therefore failing to give the teaching help needed by educationally and socially deprived children: a situation which, if unchecked, could only increase antagonism on the grounds that coloured pupils were holding back the educational progress of white pupils.

We treated it as an emergency operation and mobilized all the resources we could to teach Asian pupils with language difficulties in small groups of from four to six. First of all, and most important, was what we as a staff could do. Timetable arrangements were made to enable a staff team to see groups of pupils for two, three, or five periods a week. The aim was to ensure that every one of the Asian pupils in these groups would know one member of the staff whom he would see in the group lessons and to whom he could go during the week for extra work. Teachers volunteered for this and gave up 'free' periods for the work. They were not all language specialists: besides a German teacher and two English teachers, there were teachers from the PE, geography, home economics, commerce, maths and art departments.

The willingness to do this, indeed the positive enthusiasm, came from the feeling that we were doing something about a situation that had appeared terrifying in the speed with which it had developed. It had been placed in a teaching context of more manageable proportions, and associated with aims that restored confidence. The operation had two aims. First, to break up the concentration of immigrant pupils in the lower streams. Second, not just to restore the remedial department but to strengthen it so as to lead to an improvement in the quality of the educational opportunities offered to the less able.

Thus, as soon as improvement was shown in language, however slight, Asian pupils were moved into higher streams. The language work was pursued on a group basis in English lessons and also through withdrawal to the groups taught by the staff team: the organization of this became the responsibility of the remedial department. The argument for rapid movement to higher streams was that intelligent Asian pupils were more likely to encounter situations within the class that encouraged them to speak English. However, this meant that all teachers, not just the remedial or the emergency staff team, had to remember that language was their concern whatever their subject. Discussions were held in all departments, and these concentrated upon how in their particular lessons they could help Asian pupils to acquire a vocabulary that would make them more at home in the school.

With the majority of Asian pupils moved into forms of higher ability, the policy proved to be successful; but with a small number the move put too great a demand upon them. I now believe that there were three reasons for this. Firstly, in our anxiety to improve their command of English and to integrate them into the school community, we paid insufficient attention to the social and emotional education needed. Secondly, we failed to give these few pupils enough support by a group of teachers, acting as counsellors and language tutors: this is understandable in view of the number of pupils being taught by the staff team. Thirdly, and perhaps more important, we had thrust them into a situation and not properly considered its implications for our teaching methods. Nevertheless, as I have already said, with the majority it was successful, and showed that we need not accept a situation where Indian and West Indian pupils were consigned to the 'bottom' streams.

Help was also sought outside the school. The local authority's remedial teaching service helped in two ways. Peripatetic teachers came to teach reading to small groups of remedial pupils, English and West Indian; but this we considered as a temporary measure until we first rescued and then strengthened the remedial department. The greatest help came to be the regular contact we had with the service acting as advisers. They brought into the school materials, equipment, and ideas from other areas facing similar problems. We also contacted local colleges of education, and from one of them a group of students came on two days a week to help. From these we recruited a teacher for our remedial department; originally he had intended to teach economics to examination pupils – he is now head of a remedial department in a secondary school with a large proportion of immigrant pupils.

Out of this response to meet a situation that was seen as almost a disaster for the school came a number of benefits.

The remedial department was strengthened: it developed a strong group of specialist teachers, there was a greater range of materials and equipment, and it enjoyed greater prestige within the school and amongst the staff.

The cooperative effort had brought together specialists and it had led them to consider a common teaching problem rather than narrow questions of their own particular subject. This encouraged the development of a team approach in other areas of the curriculum.

We were led to examine the educational effects of rigidly streamed forms, particularly on those consigned to the lower ability streams. The success of the remedial department made us question previously held beliefs about the necessity of forming homogeneous teaching groups. Increasingly teaching methods made more use of group and individual learning. All this led to the relaxation of the streamed organization and towards non-streamed teaching groups.

The biggest gain was that more teachers – and not just remedial specialists – were forced to examine the relationship between language and learning.

Our first assumptions were: (a) that the only language problem was with Asian pupils and that this was simply the problem of teaching a second language; (b) that English pupils in the remedial streams were there because of low intelligence, and this manifested itself in reading difficulties and an impoverished vocabulary; (c) that West Indian pupils spoke English, so if they experienced learning difficulties it was simply because they were less intelligent or had a poor attitude towards work.

Under pressure of experience such a simple and complacent shield would not hold. The difficulties experienced in speech, in writing and in reading were *the same* for some English pupils as for West Indian. Indeed, once manifestly intelligent Indian pupils mastered the rudiments of English, many of the difficulties they encountered in academic work were also related to similar language problems. The truth had to be faced that for very many of our pupils the English we used in our lessons was nearly as incomprehensible as a foreign language.

In order to decide how best to cultivate an improvement in language, we had to establish its importance within the curriculum. A staff conference was held on the subject, and discussions went on within subject departments. The thoroughness of the examination and the effectiveness of the action taken varied, but all became more aware of the role of language. One result was a reorganization of the first-year curriculum so that teams of teachers could more easily arrange the kinds of educational experience that cultivate the growth of language. We also had to make renewed efforts to understand the cultural background of our pupils, English and the children of immigrant parents. Often the biggest surprises came from the handicaps that English pupils brought along with their reluctant steps as they came to the school.

This last concern was closely related to what we had seen as the second major problem posed by the influx of coloured pupils: their integration into the school community in order to anticipate and prevent the growth of prejudice and tensions. When the numbers were small there had been no obvious problem: the few naturally found friends and interests within the school. Now there were visible coteries and gangs of coloured pupils speaking their own language, clearly marked off from white pupils. To us, this was a situation fraught with possible tensions, especially in an area known for its gangs and their fights.

One area of mixing was on the games field. As the pupils always had their game periods in year blocks, it was possible to encourage team games that mixed the races even when we still had 'streamed' forms with a heavy concentration of black pupils in the lower stream. The school had always prided itself on its hockey teams, and the arrival of Indian boys strengthened the teams: here was one obvious means for a contribution to the life of the school. Nevertheless, it is possible to exaggerate the influence of sport in promoting racial understanding; it can often do the opposite. The true test is whether the organized integration of the games periods is followed in the unorganized games played during lunch time. This was very slow to happen, and racial groups noticeably kept to themselves.

The other area, of course, was in the various club activities, and steps were taken to encourage black pupils to join these activities. An Indian Club was formed by some of the senior pupils, and this helped not merely to introduce extra-curricula activities but also to assist newly arrived pupils to adjust to the school. Indian and West Indian arts were introduced into the crafts, music and drama clubs; in particular, Indian dances became a very popular feature of school concerts. But once again, difficulties should not be minimized. Unfortunately, the vast majority of our black pupils lived outside the nominal catchment area of the school. Within the estate that surrounded the school racial prejudice could easily be exploited, and this resulted at times in acts of hostility towards black pupils walking through the estate to attend various extra-curricula activities. This, in turn, provoked retaliation from groups of older black youths. As far as possible we attempted to anticipate difficulties, and when there were special events buses ran to the school.

The distance parents of these pupils had to travel to get to the school made it more difficult for them to take part in school functions or to be active in the parent–teacher association. Many of them, hearing stories (usually considerably exaggerated) of racial hostility in the area, were understandably not keen on their children attending school activities in the evening. They were also reluctant to come to the school themselves. It was this reluctance based upon fear that we had to overcome amongst many parents.

Their own children were the best missionaries for the school. Those who became involved in activities struggled to get the interest and support of their parents. As we sought to organize this pressure, so we discovered the manifold forms of prejudice: some of our Indian girls in the dance club were full of excuses as to why their mothers couldn't attend concerts – the real reason was that they were embarrassed by their mothers' clothes. They did not want their mothers' appearance to be yet another reminder that within the school they as Indians were 'different'.

Some older pupils were used as liaison officers, to visit homes to explain to parents what was going on in the school, and to encourage them to visit the school. The appointment by the authority of two liaison officers helped to extend systematic home

visiting, and eventually they were joined in their visiting programme by myself and some other teachers.

But once again, this was not just a problem of 'immigrants'.
Many, if not the majority, of white parents shared with black
parents a lack of understanding of what the school was about and
a reluctance to visit the school – unless they tore into it under the
momentum of a temper aroused by some 'unfairness' to their
child. The involvement of parents and of the use of home visits
concerned the relationship of the school to *all* its parents.

The question of whether racial problems should or should not
be taught never presented itself to us for the simple reason that
they already figured in a course of contemporary studies taken by
all fourth-year pupils. This was a course that had developed out
of the older, traditional social studies; but in place of a sequence
of information about the local, national and international communities, the course was organized around a number of problems. It sought to introduce pupils to those significant areas of
the human condition which made up the world they lived in:
inevitably it had to consider such problems as the position of the
family, of law and order, of welfare and poverty, of urban life
and affluence, of differences within the world. Such studies were
not taught in an abstract way but began and constantly returned
to human situations, and this involved the consideration of questions of personal responsibility and relationship.

This course was taught by a team of four teachers for between
six to eight periods a week. The word 'taught' needs some
qualification. The course was built around a number of questions
believed to be of importance to the young adolescent: who am I?
where do I come from? what are the actions I can take? why are
some to be preferred to others? The areas chosen for study were
precisely those that allowed such questions to be examined.

In a number of ways the pupils were invited to look more
carefully at their immediate situation and then helped to place it
within a wider national and international context. This inevitably raised specific problems that are central to any educational
treatment of race: what do we mean by developed and under-
developed countries? what are the roots of conflict between
people and between nations? why are some races in a superior,
social, economic and political position? Pupils had to be pre-

sented with information from history, geography, science and sociology to gain an understanding of these problems. Literature and other human studies were used to awaken imaginative insight into the human condition. Through this course of studies our pupils were already made aware of the world context of our society, and therefore of the terrible price exacted from mankind by racial intolerance.

With the arrival of large numbers of black pupils the question we faced was how to adapt the teaching approach within this course to allow for multi-racial (by which we meant black and white) discussion groups. There was never any question of not including material dealing with racialism. For young people taken from one society and plunged into another, more complex in its range of material opportunities, the questions examined in the course were even more important than to native-born pupils belonging to the racial majority. To attempt to examine them without considering the implications of race would be absurd, even more absurd in an area experiencing racial tension than in one where liberalism can remain merely an academic stance.

There were a number of features of the work experienced up to that time that encouraged us to feel that it could be tackled. The first was that the course was not organized so that world problems were a separate section; we did not envisage racialism or colour prejudice as a separate issue. The work in the various inquiries began by examining specific human situations and then led outwards to the wider context. Therefore matters of world poverty, racial prejudice and conflict would be dealt with as aspects of a number of problems of life in the world of the mid-twentieth century. This was very important when we came to examine how to present the question of immigration. By approaching it through a number of inquiries we could hope to break down the impression that it was capable of being explained through simple causes; and that therefore social difficulties attendant upon large-scale immigration were capable of a simple solution – such as 'send them back'.

The second was that work in the integrated course was beginning to influence the work in separate subjects, such as mathematics, science and home economics. The influence was twofold: either in developing skills required in the integrated course, or upon the fields of study within the separate subjects. Thus, it was possible for pupils within option groups in individual subjects, such as science, to pursue to greater depth a topic of significance to the inquiries within contemporary studies, such as a study of social anthropology in science. The aim was for the academic work in subjects to reinforce the discussion carried out in the course of contemporary studies.

The third feature was the strength of the tutor group system within the course. The team of teachers planned the course together, and where necessary could work with a complete year group. But each member of the team had a particular group of pupils and this was the tutorial where the discussion went on; throughout the year the relationship between the tutor and his group became close and very stable. The fact that the teachers were experienced, respected members of staff helped enormously.

A decision made by the team also helped: their role was not the restricted one of the authoritative source of information, and this meant they acknowledged that they were people with viewpoints and opinions, even prejudices. This is the most difficult decision facing the teacher, particularly when dealing with controversial subjects, and I have yet to know of any approach that completely overcomes the difficulty. Ours decided to be honest: to make it clear that on many issues they held opinions which were not the 'right answers', but conclusions resulting from how they interpreted the evidence.

They went even further: on some issues, such as capital punishment or the welfare state, they made it clear to pupils that honest differences of opinion existed within the team. They realized that in departing from the pedagogic security of hard facts they were inviting a backlash of prejudices from the pupils. And these prejudices would be aroused by many issues, not just colour. Their aim was to establish not that there were right and wrong answers, or even that prejudice – in the sense of an emotional commitment – is wrong (some can be socially desirable), but that there was a difference between rational opinion based upon an understanding of a situation and irrational hate fed by ignorance.

How far this was successful in the case of *racial* prejudice is difficult to assess. All that can be said is that the team had sufficient confidence to continue with the handling of controversial issues, and that much informed discussion did go on in the groups.

I believe that the approach of the team was right, and that such work opens up the possibility of introducing the study of race and colour into other areas of the secondary curriculum. But looking back I now believe that our thinking was vitiated by three mistaken attitudes.

1. 'Integration equals assimilation.'
When we talked about Indian or West Indian pupils integrating into the school community, what we really meant was that we wanted them to become English schoolboys and girls – of the nice, obedient variety, of course. In this, we were often abetted by parents without realizing the terrible, immediate strain this was putting upon many youngsters, especially those who had only recently been reunited with parents after many years. I think that this attitude still persists as witnessed by the too frequent conflicts over school uniform and the dress of Asian pupils.

There can be more serious damage to the pupils, because we are undermining their pride in their own community. Only too often it is possible to talk with intelligent young coloured people who tell you that they feel suspended between two worlds: they no longer want to belong to the world of their parents, they know they are not admitted to the world of the English for which their education prepared them and for no other world. Within our history we still teach of the vision and courage of forebears who emigrated to found an empire (with footnotes of those who went as convicts and indentured labour, or because of land clearances and famine); but the parents of these young people are more usually referred to as our immigration problem. Such an approach can produce people ashamed of their own race: but as the history of nationalist movements shows, the reaction can be equally as violent.

Within the curriculum itself there were three major errors resulting from this first mistake. Firstly, we concentrated upon teaching how to speak and write English without due attention to the complex problems of cultural background. Secondly, we failed to distinguish between the various races: they were all 'immigrants'. Of course, we lacked the knowledge to recognize or do anything about the racial and cultural differences; but more significant was that we didn't even ask the right question. Thirdly, despite the songs and dances in school concerts, we did not make use of cultural diversity within the curriculum.

2. 'Prejudice should not exist.'

We sought to underplay the importance of race and to emphasize the importance of our common humanity. This meant that in teaching situations we were frightened of prejudice, treating it as unnatural. Perhaps a better starting point for our thinking is to accept prejudice as a natural, normal feature of life, not as something introduced by alien, outside forces.

We might then recognize race as being an important factor influencing our lives. National pride is not the right of the linguist and racialist. A multi-racial society needs a pride in race and a recognition of distinctive racial contributions. This is not at variance with an education for world citizenship.

Of course, there is the danger of accentuating racial differences; but that danger is there now and will continue so long as people feel threatened by 'strangers'. We cannot ignore racial and cultural differences; understanding demands that they be recognized.

3. 'Too late and too little.'

Our response to the introduction of a sizeable proportion of black pupils was limited to two areas: one, the teaching of the English language; two, the humanities curriculum of the fourth- and fifth-year pupils. This is not enough.

Once a school begins to consider how controversial issues can be introduced into the education of young adolescents, then inevitably the entire curriculum of the secondary school comes under review. Demands are made upon the knowledge, the skills and the attitudes fourth-year pupils need to bring to the work, and this means a reshaping of the curriculum in the first three years.

This is being experienced in all our secondary schools, but nowhere is the need more urgent than in those faced with the question of what kind of an education should we provide in schools which are multi-racial communities. Colour adds a new dimension to our educational needs; it is not something that can be dealt with by adding on some special courses or providing a package of relevant materials, although they would give some help.

This account has dealt with the situation of some years ago, when the problem was that of dealing with large numbers of pupils recently arrived in this country. Today the question is what are the demands upon the secondary schools of coloured pupils who have been educated in our primary schools, and who see this country as their home country? Therefore much I have said already belongs to a past situation; but some of the major points still apply. Our curriculum is still very largely a ragbag of an extremely insular education. Even where we teach some aspects of world affairs they are still firmly within the world of Mercator's projection: we look outwards from a Britain in the centre of a world crossed by the Victorian shipping routes. The history of other parts of the world begins with the arrival of Western European colonizers, despite the occasional recognition of the Aztec or the Inca. Civilization, as taught in our present curriculum, is something carried in the holds of the European ships, not a continuing venture by the races of mankind.

What is taught in our schools – the history, literature, religion, science, geography – all needs to be looked at to discover the kind of eyes we are giving to our pupils to look at the world. It is impossible for secondary pupils to leave school with an adequate understanding of the nature of their century unless they have an awareness of the social, economic, political, and moral consequences of the expansion of Western Europe since 1500. Too much still remains of the approach that tells it as a story with the moral that the Englishman is worth two Frenchmen and in arithmetical ratio to other races as we move towards the equator; equally, it is wrong to replace this with an account of mean-spirited greed and cruelty of which we should be ashamed.

Our pupils deserve an understanding of what went on and is going on from both sides of the hill, of the interaction of different societies and cultures, of the range of choices seen by people as possible to them, of the consequences of decisions. If our pupils are to live successfully in a complex society, within which race relations will be a dominant (if not *the* dominant) problem, then it is essential that they be given an understanding of the complexities of human life, society and actions. A curriculum of prepared pap, whether from a 'reactionary' or 'progressive' source, is an inadequate diet.

What is suggested is not just a new approach to the teaching of history; far from it, it has implications for all subjects and areas of the curriculum. Let us examine the central feature of colonial expansion: slavery and its manifold forms. Can we be satisfied that its importance in world history receives adequate recognition in education? And yet this was an accepted condition of life for hundreds of millions, either as slave or beneficiary, throughout history; and in a variety of ways still persists. It is difficult to grasp the social and psychological position of people in the present world without an appreciation of the consequences of slavery, for masters as well as for slaves.

This is not just a question for teachers of history and geography. It lies at the very heart of the question of evil, and we cannot escape from this in our approach to religious education and literature. An examination of people's attitudes towards it plunges us into questions of scientific evidence and the scientific method when applied to racial differences, whether real or imagined. Questions of the application of technology (already being introduced into the curriculum) lead back to how societies view people: as units of production or human beings with inalienable rights? Above all, it must lead into a consideration of people and how they are viewed. This can relate present situations with the past in a variety of ways: a comparison of the Jew of history with the modern Israeli; of the stage Irishman with the Kennedys.

A recognition of race within our curriculum does not imply the construction of specific courses to 'teach' about the evils of racialism and the good of racial tolerance. It needs to inform a re-thinking of our secondary-school curriculum to produce an education more realistic to and adequate for the society our pupils are entering. It can deal with questions of race in a variety of ways, lively and imaginative, and conducive to the encouragement of rational thought by pupils.

For such a reshaping to succeed, two conditions must be met. First, there must be teachers of quality and imagination; second, they must work in ways that develop a stable and confident teacher–pupil relationship. We need teachers who can help pupils to frame questions capable of rational investigation, and this can only be done when teachers work together over a period of time. All our schools need this, but none more than those with a multi-racial population; yet nowhere are the staffing problems so acute.

Schools with large numbers of coloured pupils tend to be in inner-ring urban areas; tend to be in the older buildings; tend to have the greatest difficulty in attracting teachers. Our educational system perpetuates inequality behind the façade of equality of opportunity. A building programme designed to put roofs over heads means that most new schools are in expanding residential areas that attract the socially mobile, more favoured sections of the population. Capitation and teaching allowances are geared to the unit total of the school, a 'fair' system based upon numbers and ages of pupils. In practice, it means that the school with the large sixth form, normally in the better-off residential areas, can offer bigger allowances for key staff (usually teachers who will spend most of their time with the academically able), has a greater sum to spend on stock, and will offer a greater range of opportunities.

This is a generalization, but despite the efforts of some authorities to give more to the depressed areas it is true enough that more is needed to correct the disparity of educational provision. Key posts in schools in deprived areas must compare favourably with the most fortunate of our grammar and comprehensives; indeed it could be argued that the financial inducement should be greater. Money over and above the normal capitation and grants should be available to the heads of such schools to increase educational opportunities. This requires not just action by government and local authorities, but also a willingness by teacher organizations to negotiate local anomalies within national agreements.

Multi-racial schools must be given the material and intellectual encouragement to become community schools. This will mean that teachers, administrators, councillors (and ministers of state) realize what they mean when they talk about a 'good' school. One cannot aim at a community school and use the criteria of success nurtured in the grammar school of the 'best end' of town. These were institutions established to take 'clever boys of the neighbourhood' and to educate them in a self-contained community. There are those who worry that any departure from this means a loss of 'standards'. Equally worrying is that the maintenance of these 'standards' when applied in our 'good' schools had meant failure for so many. For too many pupils, especially in socially deprived areas, they are not standards to be attained but terms of servitude and inferiority.

Perhaps the involvement of the community is essential precisely because standards need to be raised. Earlier I pointed to our failure to recognize the importance of cultural diversity within our curricula planning. This is not to argue that each culture demands its own education. There is one education that we must offer to all our pupils, not different kinds for different categories; but we need to widen considerably the way into that education. There is not just one cultural background that provides a fruitful starting point, and there isn't just one set of attitudes that will prove a desirable result.

Such an approach is essential within a multi-racial school; but not just there. It isn't only the coloured pupils who suffer from an inadequate secondary curriculum; I would say this is true for the majority of our pupils, especially the socially deprived. The question of language and of its relationship to the cultural background is central to the attempt to improve the quality of the education provided for all our pupils. So too, the rethinking of the curriculum to provide an adequate education for a multi-racial society is not the problem of schools with coloured pupils: it should be the concern of us all.

9 Race and the Teacher: An Idiosyncratic Bibliography

A. Sivanandan

How the teacher sees the child is how the child sees itself. 'One of the unfortunate aspects of urban education is that middle-class teachers too often expect too little from the children of the poor. In the case of the black poor, low expectations are often inter-mingled with racism.'* Cultural differences, while compounding this tendency, provide, at the same time, a ready-made rationale for racism.

How some of these notions of racial superiority arose during the colonial period of European history is told in V. G. Kiernan's *Lords of Human Kind: European Attitudes in the Imperial Age* (Weidenfeld & Nicolson, 1969). But to understand the effect of such attitudes on the colonized, one must turn to Frantz Fanon's *Black Skin, White Masks* (Paladin, 1970). Himself a (black) psychiatrist, Fanon shows how colonialism served to undermine the 'native's' sense of identity and of self-worth and to remove from him all control over his own destiny – aspects of personality which, on the showing of the Coleman Report,† 'the most extensive educational study ever conducted', are crucial to a child's aspirations and achievement.

It was the active acknowledgement of this fact in the work he did and, arising from his work, the indictment he made of a bigoted schools system, that earned for Jonathan Kozol his dis-missal from a Boston school. But he has since told his tale in *Death at an Early Age* (Penguin, 1968). More recently a group of teachers in Harlem got their children to write of their world as they saw it – in any form they wished, and to hell with grammar. The result, published under the title *The Me Nobody*

---

* Maurice R. Berube, 'Educational achievement and community control', *Community Issues*, vol. 1, no. 1, November 1968.

† 'Equality of educational opportunity', National Center for Educational Statistics, Washington, D.C., 1966.

Knows: Children's Voices from the Ghetto, and edited by
Stephen M. Joseph (New York, Avon, 1970), is sometimes
literature, often philosophy, but always the poignant sociology of
the ghetto. From the ghetto, too, comes the autobiography of a
man who more than any other single figure in recent history has
given back to black children everywhere a sense of their own
worth and dignity: *The Autobiography of Malcolm X*, edited by
Alex Haley (Penguin, 1970).

Tales of black ghetto life in Britain are still to be published. So
far, only Augustine John's report on Handsworth, *Race in the
Inner City* (Runnymede Trust, 1970), has even attempted
to delineate the black condition. But the 'noli me tangere' attitude that the book has evoked among teachers bodes ill for
anyone who cares to tell it 'like it is'. More acceptable, possibly,
are the tales of rejection and disaffection experienced by West
Indians on their arrival in the 'mother country'. One such book is
Donald Hinds's *Journey to an Illusion* (Heinemann, 1966).
Another, the story of a skilled craftsman who finally moved on,
disillusioned, is Wallace Collins's *Jamaican Migrant* (Routledge
& Kegan Paul, 1965).

The novels of many West Indian writers such as George Lam-
ming, Samuel Selvon and Andrew Salkey further illuminate the
picture of a people caught between two worlds.

In a vein more analytical, though not without anecdote, is the
Vicious Circle of Wilfred Wood and John Downing (SPCK,
1968). It tells of the historical and socio-economic background of immigration to Britain (particularly West Indian immigration) and examines the 'societal pressures' that devolve on
coloured 'immigrants' on arrival. More specifically, Marina
Maxwell describes these pressures in terms of schooling in an
article in the September 1969 issue of *Race Today**: 'Violence
in the toilets: the experiences of a black teacher in Brent
schools'.

The Asian experience, however, is even less well documented.
To enter into the mind of the Asian child, one must turn away
from the trite exercises in sociology (readily found in the bibliography on *Coloured Immigrants in Britain†*) and look at the folk

---

*Institute of Race Relations, monthly, 20p.

†A. Sivanandan, Institute of Race Relations, 1969, £1.05.

tales of the Indian sub-continent, such as Kushwant Singh's *Land of the Five Rivers: Stories from the Punjab* (Bombay, Jaico, 1965), Sarla Jagmohan's *Selected Stories from Gujarat* (Bombay, Jaico, 1961), Ghosh's *Tales from Indian Classics* (Bombay, Jaico, 1965). From these one would gather how the religious elements of Indian and Pakistani life are closely bound up with their socio-cultural outlook. For an understanding of their religions, then, one needs to turn to *East comes West: A Background to some Asian Faiths* by Peggy Holroyde and others (CRC, 1970).

The contemporary Asian novel (in English), however, is thematically more limited than its Caribbean counterpart. Prawer Jhabvala, Balachandra Rajan, Kamala Markandaya, Anand Lall and others deal mostly with the conflict of cultures among middle-class Asians as perceived in their personal relationships. Those novelists who are concerned with more varied aspects of their society are still writing in their native tongue and are rarely translated into English.

But an appraisal of attitudes and an understanding of other life styles are in themselves worthless if they are not accompanied by a knowledge of how the institutions of British society actually work *vis à vis* its coloured population. W. W. Daniel's summary of the PEP report on *Racial Discrimination in England* (Penguin, 1968), is one book which tells of attitudes in action. (There are others – and these are listed in the bibliography on coloured immigrants mentioned above.) But how successive governments in this country predicated the climate in which discrimination came to lose its shame is narrated in Paul Foot's *Immigration and Race in British Politics* (Penguin, 1965).

For a comprehensive overview of the subject, however, there is the compendious *Colour and Ctizenship: A Report on British Race Relations* by E. J. B. Rose and associates (Oxford University Press, 1969) or its more up-to-date abridgement: *Colour, Citizenship and British Society* by Nicholas Deakin and associates (Panther, 1970).

Further Reading

Douglas Barnes, James Britton and **Harold Rosen,** *Language, the Learner and the School*, Penguin, 1971, 2nd edn.

D. M. and **G. A. Gahagan,** *Talk Reform*, Routledge & Kegan Paul, 1971.

Denis Lawton, *Social Class, Language and Education*, Routledge & Kegan Paul, 1968.

John and **Elizabeth Newson,** *Patterns of Infant Care in an Urban Community*, Penguin, 1965.

John and **Elizabeth Newson,** *Four Years Old in an Urban Community*, Penguin, 1970.

Liverpool EPA Project: *Occasional papers 1-10.*

Projectors:

Social Environment and the Downtown School. An advisory booklet on social studies for 8–13 year olds.

Home–School Horse-Sense. An advisory wallet with six practical suggestions.

Streets Ahead. A social problem game for children in urban junior and secondary schools.

from K. J. Pulham, Paddington Comprehensive School, Liverpool, L7 3EA.

Leila Berg, *Risinghill: Death of a Comprehensive School*, Penguin, 1968.

Alec Clegg and **Barbara Megson,** *Children in Distress*, Penguin, 1968.

David Hargreaves, *Social Relations in a Secondary School*, Routledge & Kegan Paul, 1967.

Derek Humphry and **Gus John,** *Because They're Black*, Penguin, 1971.

George Jackson, *Soledad Brother*, Penguin, 1971.

School of Barbiana, *Letter to a Teacher*, Penguin, 1970.

Alan Sillitoe, *The Loneliness of the Long-Distance Runner*, Pan, 1968.

Department of Education Surveys:

10: *Potential and Progress in a Second Culture: A Survey of the Assessment of Pupils from Overseas*, HMSO, 1971.
13: *Education of Immigrants*, 1971.
14: *The Continuing Needs of Immigrants*, 1972.

Community Relations Commission monographs, *Education for Multi-Cultural Societies:*

1: *Syllabuses*, 1970.
2: *Language*, 1972.
3: *World Religion: Aid for Teachers*, 1972.

Multi-Racial School, journal published three times a year by Oxford University Press.

Because They're Black

Derek Humphrey and Gus John

The two authors of this book (one of them is a black social worker and the author of the Handsworth report) have managed to get black people to talk, to 'tell it like it is'. The major part of this book is devoted to careful description of what it feels like to be on the receiving end of the kind of discrimination nearly every one of us exercises. We even *look* at black people differently, as if they were freaks. In this description is laid bare the way in which the barriers of mutual incomprehension have come to be.

The last section of the book is devoted to the way out. Integration is discussed and shown for what it is: the desire to convert black men into white men. Black power, different in kind but as strong as its US counterpart, is seen as a humanizing necessity, not only for blacks but for whites too. Political conflict and struggle are essential if we are to change ourselves and our society sufficiently to see not only black men as human but to make ourselves human too.

The appendix by Dr Hashmi on the psychology of racial prejudice shows how those who are finally less than human are those infected by the disease.

Children in Distress

Alec Clegg and Barbara Megson

Two out of every hundred children have to be given direct help by the State – whether it be psychiatric, social or medical.

But are these the only children 'in distress'? What about those children who do not qualify for State help?

Alec Clegg and Barbara Megson estimate that perhaps 12 per cent of our children desperately need help, but do not qualify to receive it. *Children in Distress* paints an agonizing picture of child distress, based on the authors' long experience in educational administration. They argue that it is the schools – in daily contact with the children – that are the agencies best suited to help this large and saddening section of our child population.

'. . . this book, containing a wealth of information and ideas based on the experience of very many schools, can help teachers who want to help their problem pupils, but just do not know how to start. It can help them, probably more than any other single volume.' – *The Times Educational Supplement*

Language, the Learner and the School
Revised edition

Douglas Barnes, James Britton, Harold Rosen and the LATE

Language is the most subtle and pervasive of the means by which we present our assumptions about role, about subject-matter, and about the people we talk to, at and with. And yet, as Douglas Barnes's fascinating survey of secondary-school classrooms shows, teachers tend to talk too much (and pupils too little), and are often also insensitive to the effects and significance of the language they use and expect. What can we learn about learning by looking at the language of our classrooms?

Douglas Barnes's research was aimed at finding some answers to this important question. James Britton's contribution switches attention to the pupil: what function does talk have – even ordinary, undemanding, trivial talk for talk's sake – in the development of thought. This revised edition contains a new version of the 'discussion document', designed to bring together teachers of all subjects in a common 'language policy' within the school, and an account by Harold Rosen of the work going on in schools directly instigated by the first edition of this book.

Letter to a Teacher
School of Barbiana

Afterword by Lord Boyle of Handsworth

Eight young Italian boys from the mountains outside Florence wrote this passionate and eloquent book. It took them a year. Simply and clearly, with some devastating statistical analysis of the Italian education system, they set out to show the ways in which attitudes towards class, behaviour, language and subject-matter militate against the poor. They describe, too, the reforms they propose, and the methods they use in their own school – the School of Barbiana, started under the guidance of a parish priest and now run entirely by the children.

This remarkable book was written for the parents of the Italian poor. But it is about the poor everywhere: their anger is the anger of every worker and peasant who sees middle-class children absorbed effortlessly into the schools as teacher's favourites.

Letter to a Teacher was a best-seller in Italy and has been published subsequently in many languages. The School of Barbiana was awarded the prize of the Italian Physical Society, usually reserved for promising physicists, for the statistical achievement involved in the book.

' ... this marvel of a book ... a masterpiece of protest ... an original work of Literature ... I have read no book on education that has left me so uncomfortably aware of the injustice done daily in our schools to great masses of our fellow human beings.' – *Edward Blishen*

Risinghill: Death of a Comprehensive School

Leila Berg

'Wild school is tamed by love'

'Does sparing the rod breed crime?'

'Parents will fight move to close school'

The school which produced these headlines in 1964 and 1965 was Risinghill, a co-educational comprehensive in Islington.
This is its story, told often in the words of pupils and parents, the story of its courageous headmaster, Michael Duane, and the story of its eventual closure. It is a passionate indictment of educational bureaucracy and bureaucrats, of intolerance and stupidity. It is a story in which the word 'love' occurs again and again, in neither a sentimental nor a titillating way, but as a key word in a basic conflict about the state education of children. It is a sad story, written in anger and without fear.

36 Children

Herbert Kohl

Herbert Kohl's 36 children were black twelve year olds in New York's Harlem. From their standpoint school was an irrelevance, to be treated sometimes with humour, sometimes with lethargy, sometimes with dull, impotent, insolent anger. From the standpoint of the educational establishment they were 'the unteachable'. Herbert Kohl was their teacher.

His achievement was to gain the confidence of his children and to demonstrate that the world was more open to them than their ghetto surroundings might suggest. Their innate exuberance and liveliness come through in the series of writings and drawings which form a major part of this book. As Herbert Kohl makes clear, the process of educating necessitated profound changes in his own sense of himself as a teacher and a person. Few books on education give such an inward view of what it is like to face an impossible teaching situation and, in some measure, to come through.

'Desperate, angry, heartrending. . . . What Mr Kohl discovered during that year . . . is relevant to teaching anywhere: marvellously exciting.' Edward Blishen in the *New Statesman*